1-800-OH-MY-BLACKNESS

contemporary writs by

CHRIS BENT

www.chrisbent.com

Published in the USA by Chris Bent
Naples, Florida USA
http://ChrisBent.com

© Copyright 2016 Chris Bent. All Rights Reserved.
ISBN 978-0-9978283-2-0 (Paperback)
ISBN 978-0-9978283-3-7 (E-Book)

1-800-I-AM-UNHAPPY,
1-800-FOR-WOMEN-ONLY,
1-800-LAUGHING-OUT-LOUD,
1-800-OH-MY-GOODNESS,
1-800-FOR-SEALS-ONLY,
1-800-OH-MY-DONALD,
1-800-FOR-VETERANS-ONLY, and
1-800-ONLY-FOR-LOVE
are trademarks owned by
Chris Bent and are used with his permission.

Also By Chris Bent

Available in Paperback and Electronic Versions
at Amazon and iBooks

1-800-I-AM-UNHAPPY
Volume 1

1-800-I-AM-UNHAPPY
Volume 2

1-800-FOR-WOMEN-ONLY

1-800-LAUGHING-OUT-LOUD

1-800-OH-MY-GOODNESS

1-800-FOR-SEALS-ONLY

1-800-OH-MY-DONALD

1-800-FOR-VETERANS-ONLY

1-800-ONLY-FOR-LOVE

1-800-OH-MY-BLACKNESS

Coming Soon:

1-800-OLD-PEOPLE-MATTER

Praise for
1-800-Oh-My-Blackness

"Chris, just got finished reading your chapters. A lot to digest, but so much of it, if not all of it, point on. I'm flattered that Nancy thinks this highly of me to offer you my opinion. What stuck out the most in the reading was values and respectability. I try to teach the young people I mentor the three "Rs", reliability, respectability, and responsibility.

Adam Bomb was the bomb, I hope I'm hunched over with pride helping others."

Harold G Weeks, President, NAACP Collier County, Naples, FL

"Chris, I am a black man... better stated, I am a man in black skin. You capture and present a view of the uncolored spirit that lives inside. You have captured the unique way to challenge the heart with the eyes, the eyes with the morals, the soul with the flesh and essence of survival with eventual death if we continue to turn a blind eye to the truth that screams for change. The eyes that read this book will be forever changed. The mind will question. Long established misconceptions will be reevaluated. And hopefully change how we view, treat and learn from those born with differences."

Vernon K. Jackson

More Praise for Chris Bent's Writing

"Paradox is a person that combines contradictory features. Chris Bent is a paradox. Reading his most recent works I am not surprised by the depth, humor, passion and spirituality. In spite of mixed content the flow between chapters allows you to enjoy the paradox. Chris' muses have caused a few smiles; some ponderings and touched my heart. Let this Paradox of a Man walk up to you and continue the conversation.

Nancy Lascheid, RN, BSN, Co-Founder,
Neighborhood Health Clinic, Naples, Florida

"One need only look into the night sky to recognize that there is brilliance in chaos. One need only read this book to realize the same. Intertwined in stories, random thoughts, and opinions one will find extraordinary pearls of wisdom in here..........and a lot of them. Chris is brilliant."

Navy SEAL Commander

"Dear Frogfather, Your writings remind me of the lessons and examples that were taught to me and my siblings by my parents, grandparents and the nuns that taught me in parochial school. I am so blessed to have them in my life. We are also blessed to have you because you have taken the time and effort to put down in writing your thoughts. They are insightful, and positive, to help us lead a better life. Thank you."

Maureen Murphy, Mother of LT. Michael Murphy, Medal of Honor recipient, BUD/S Class 236, SDVT-1

More reviews of Chris Bent's books can be found in the "In The Words Of Others" section at the back of this book.

DEDICATION

To Christina, Candice, Courtney, Vickie and their journeys . . .

Prologue

This is meant to be a book for just one person. If just that one person is touched in some way to make their journey better, then the effort is not in vain. Each one of us can look back to one moment that changed our direction for the better. May this book, a collection of my writs and wit, find that pair of eyes.

Chris Bent

Kennebunkport
August 2016
www.ChrisBent.com

Contents

Chapters

White Chalk

White chalk.

Blackboards.

Not that many years ago.

We all learned on black and white.

Black and white watched the teacher write their names on the blackboard with white chalk on the first day of classes. Math, history, physics, English. Truth was the catalyst. We felt it.

Except there were white schools and there were black schools. Everyone had white chalk. Black fingers had white all over them.

Courageous leaders forced integration. The symbolic chant was "There is no color."

You have to have black to write on.

Or, black type is needed to write Truths on white paper.

One is worthless without the other.

Grey chalk on blackboards makes it harder to tell the truth. It just

Black fingers had white all over them.

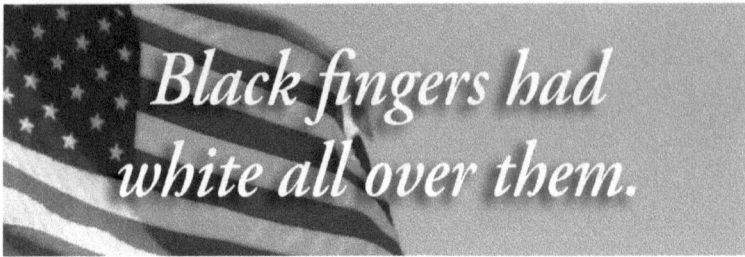

is not as clear. It wasn't about feelings. You have to get the black and white on the board or you have nothing to go by.

They say we all started from Adam and Eve. Regardless of their color, this world formed and grew on many continents with many variables which would shape the color and cultures of all ancestors. Forget the evolution debate, we are not taking issue with that here....

Then, with great insight, someone decided that black should really be green. Logical? And white chalk should be yellow or whatever. Easier on the eyes they say. Here we are playing with color again. Really? All the great minds of today, well, the older ones, never saw a green board and their eyesight is fine....

OK. I get it... or do I? We have made calling things black and white judgmental. The new truth is feelings, which must be protected at all costs.

You have to be careful labelling something as right or as wrong.

There are many opinions and each must be respected. Except that this ultimately leads to chaos.

Hello world, good and evil do exist.

We had better put both back up on the blackboards and define again which is which before it is too late.

Why is the number one selling book black?

Hey R.J., is it ok to use white chalk on a green board?

In Dignity

Black male teacher.

White female student.

First day.

She asks him what his qualifications are.

He senses the undercurrent, the underpinnings.

Class begins, we move on as if nothing is still going on.

This has been a tough week in Charleston. Forgiveness was the only way out. Heroes and saints died that day. The President's eloquence became our tear. United again for however briefly.

Dignity comes from respecting the other. Dignity comes from celebrating color while not seeing it. Oh My Blackness should be the canvas of all. As we celebrate sensitivities and diversity, somehow race is given a pass. Yet race is screaming at us from all corners. In dignity we should accept our mistakes and find a uniting focus. There is a message in Charleston.

Every classroom should discuss this tragedy. Every classroom should dissect the congregation's response. Are there values lost?

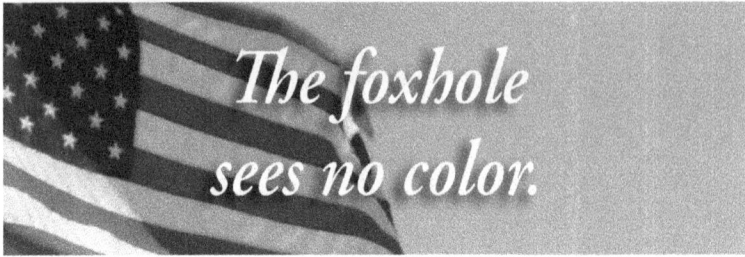

The foxhole sees no color.

Should we not reprioritize? Should there not be a class on values? At least a semester? Only educated fools contend otherwise. Separation of what? Existence and non-existence?

My friend, this teacher, turns his cheek every day as the struggle for color blindness is pursued. Maybe we can give all white people black Seeing Eye dogs? Maybe we can give all black people white Seeing Eye dogs? Huuuhh?

In dignity white hands should shake a black hand every day. This has gone on far too long. What ever happened to the United Fingers of America?

We are better than this.

WWII, Vietnam, Afghanistan, Iraq put these fingers together.

The foxhole sees no color.

Any color gives its life for any color.

Let's get our youth in a foxhole.

In Dignity.

Reflections of a Black Teacher

I have a friend who is a teacher.

He is black too.

Or should I say I have a friend who is black and happens to be a teacher.

I have other black friends. Or should I just say I have friends? I have no Muslim friends. Why should having friends be complicated?

Now this friend is peculiar as he should be writing a book I want entitled "Reflections of A Black Teacher." But he won't because he is too insecure. Not, "not ready," just insecure.

He and I have traded e-mails regarding what I have been writing and his responses come from some other world. Really sensitive and insightful. But they are coming from his perspective. I did not grow up black, so he talks and thinks with different metaphors and images. It is like a different language.

We all grow up in our own worlds and many never see the

Then there is poverty.

world or life from any other perspective much distant from our self-centered one. Being a teacher is not easy and certainly is politically charged these days. Being a black teacher adds another dimension of double political correctness.

I want my friend to get off his posterior and write the book that he already has written.

We students, teachers, administrators, politicians, and general populace could use a personal journey through the maze of feelings experienced in his journey. Celebrities get to tell all. Why can't we? Are we less boring???

Sometimes I want to respond to his musings that he is a reverse racist by all too often casting observations through a race tinted lens. But hey, when am I not judging through my establishment eyes? Like all the time.

I have been in the military where there really is no color. Who cares what the color of the guy next to you is when he may be the one who saves your life by taking your bullet?

I can think that my friend has been in an administrative combat zone, where the bureaucracy of education often protects the weak at the expense of the brave. Where a union might have it backwards. Where a school board might be lost in correctness.

Suppose you had to stand up in front of a school board and just be "not" black?

Now there is the world of the student who comes from the perfect parents without any bias. That comes from a loving mother and father who embrace and guide her with assurance and discipline. Yes, this is the norm. Well… Except that many fathers are no-show or never-showed guys.

Then there is poverty.

Then there is the entitlement mindset parent.

Does the teacher have any idea of what healing might be needed?

Of what bias the kid brings to the classroom?

We do not have a lens into their minds or baggage.

A really smart teacher knows and deals with this daily. He knows that values are the only way out; that values must be taught with strictness. Painful but necessary. Not just necessary, but absolutely essential. But it is not politically correct to do so.

Values are associated with religion. Religion is a bias. Religion is an imposition on the freedom of thinking. Game over. A sophisticated and caring teacher walks the career-ending tightrope as they try to impart more than just the schoolbook to their class.

Sneak in a little manners.

Sneak in a little unselfishness story.

Sneak in a little success story.

Sneak in a little story of hope.

Sneak in an Olympian's success where with hard, impossible work miracles do exist.

I want my buddy to write his "Reflections of a Black Teacher".

That is why this white old man wrote this.

Qualifications

Are you qualified?

To carry a weapon?

To have an opinion?

Or an impression?

Or just a curiosity?

Who has the experience and wisdom and humility and integrity to judge someone else?

Nobody. Wait one….

Some decisions do have to be made to insure the safety and future of all. Period.

District attorney. Supreme Court. All judge and are charged to create light in our heart of darkness. Authority figures do prove fallible and hypocritical. Yet… without authority there is chaos.

We have to judge. It is all in the quality and rightness. Right?

What is a teacher who hasn't studied and been "degreed"? Why does a student go into a classroom other than to learn? Should

Are you qualified?

a student disrespect the teacher? The height of pomposity and ignorance. How dumb is proven. Stay after class. Get extra homework. Oops, not politically correct…. Hmmm…

Maybe there is a hidden societal breakdown as authority is treated more and more with indifference. The new norm. Chaos.

How does a black teacher feel if a white female student questions his qualifications? The hidden sensitivities of race are thrown into the equation. Gender and race. Tricky mix. King Freeze!

Does she know the button she may be pressing? Does this ignorance of youth feed volatility, feed fact-spin, and feed self-serving half-truth? All are potential violence triggers.

What races through the black mind is 10 times that of the white. Centuries of passed-down tales of injustice and painful anticipations.

Color blindness abandoned in racial squints.

It takes a great teacher to move forward.

It takes a great teacher to respectfully admonish disrespect.

Suppose he was black too??

Starting Line

"Runners to the blocks."

"Ready."

"Set."

GUN...... Go!!!

That's how life kinda starts as we take our first breath. Kinda...

We are born with outside color. "The skin effect".

Underneath this surface is the same anatomy, blood, heart, muscles, brain. All of us are the same. All of us came from sperm and egg to fetus in our mother's womb. Life started the same. Skin color was predetermined thousands of generations ago.... Kinda...

Now comes the most powerful determinant of future well-being, the behavior of the parent. Attitude of white, attitude of black. The seeds are planted as the child scrutinizes every detail of parent behavior. Good kids can come from poverty. Bad kids can come from wealth.

Values are either taught or lost. Respect is either taught or lost.

We are born with outside color.

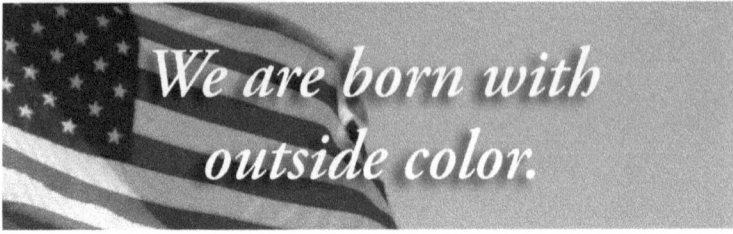

I sure wish military service was ahead for all…. But that is another story…

I grew up seeing no color. Not even knowing it was so unnecessarily tension driven. Media avoided it other than the unavoidable, like the MLK assassination….

Today that flag is being lowered across the nation. Symbolic of the challenge still ahead while not yet finding the solution.

We were a value driven nation at one point. Yes there was racism then and it still exists today.

We still look away from the obvious solution. We think regulations are the answer.

The only way out of this mire is reassessing values, and values are no longer politically correct in our schools and homes. The ones most taught are from the chaos of social networks.

The sprint to equality has been turned into a marathon. We have allowed it as we pursued entertainment and self-gratification. Not everybody, but enough to possibly bring this nation down.

The emptiness felt with a loss of hope is invisibly fueling the enormous cancer of substance abuse. Evil money creating evil. We look away. Why?

There is no black and there is no white if you grow up.

There is little crime in some neighborhoods. Some black neighborhoods too. Find out why.

I think values might be being taught there.

I think there might be singing on Sunday mornings there.

Why?

Hope?

From where?

Finish line.

Checkered flag.

Hmmm…why are they all same size black and white checks?

Parentdise Lost

When was paradise lost?

John Milton tried to make it clear with 10,000 lines of verse.

What eluded him, and us, is our own fall from grace from ourselves.

Our choice is our choice. We make a choice. We can choose to be lazy about a choice. We can choose to not seek advice on our choice.

To choose or not to choose is the question.

We can choose to ignore the obvious.

We can choose to call evil just an "issue".

We can choose to call selfishness a "need" because of "feelings".

We can choose to blame racism.

We choose today to blame everything but our selves.

Satan did his thing. Adam and Eve did theirs.

When you fall in love you momentarily taste of paradise. Your

It is just about parenting.

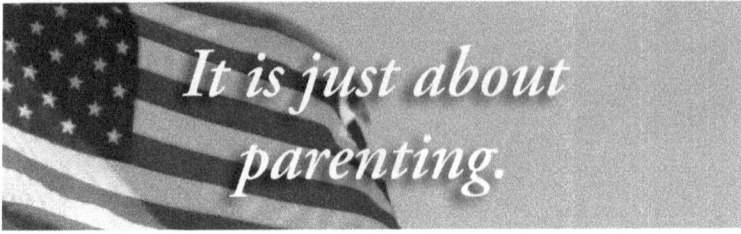

self is unimportant. The only thing that matters is the one loved. Paradise.

As children we watch to see how love is respected. How we are loved. As this leads to how we will love.

Parentdise is a pure world for most infants. If the parent is unusually good, the child will learn respect for feelings and for rules. But parents have to choose to be good. To right wrongs that may have been done to them. It is not about race. It is just about parenting.

Yet the black parent has been handed statistics that few wish to look at. Fathers disappear. Children are schooled by the grammar of the street. The gang becomes the father. Satan rules. All choices made are bad ones. Futures obliterated.

Values have been dismissed. Discipline is no longer allowed. A kid can complain about a parent or teacher and guess who is guilty until proven innocent?

If the family is broken, if the dad is gone... who is being taught what for the next generation?

Churches teach values, justice, and unselfish love. These are the answers that have been tragically labelled as being excessive and right wing.

Satan wins.

Blackjack.

Parentdise lost.

Courage Rocks

We all had to have them.

If you didn't you were not cool.

If you did you were as stupid as your Pet Rock.

What better pet than one that requires no food, doesn't bite, and lets you love it??

Most of the rocks were grey, not black... color doesn't matter with a rock anyway.

Loving a rock could not be demonized by the conservatives or the liberals.

I think we need to unite behind things that can't be criticized by minority groups or self-appointed judges.

Let's do this again. Pick any rock from the ground and we will call it our "Courage Rock". As soon as I finish the packaging we can sell them for $4.00! The proceeds will go to getting as many young men as possible off the streets and into the military. Groans... I hear them... Too bad. It is the only place left where one learns the power of discipline. Where rules save lives and futures.

We all had to have them.

It takes courage to follow the rules, it takes courage to learn how to safely fire a gun, and it takes courage to face the enemy.
It takes courage to take the street out of a kid. It takes courage to be a real dad.

A rock can have value. We sure need them to reconnect with our lost values. Those rocks that were the foundation of our Constitution and family. It takes courage not to dismiss values as folly. To say no to evil.

Yes, a Courage Rock should be in every pocket to remind us that only we can make our parents proud and our country strong again.

I'm still working on the final packaging.

I think it will be the American flag.

And I think I will scratch a small Cross on each rock.

Just for luck….

Beethoven's 5th

He made them lie down on the floor.

And close their eyes.

Since when is a floor a classroom they said?

Today's classrooms are abuzz with students at desks doing everything but studying. Secretly texting when the teacher's eyes are elsewhere. Secretly thinking of what they are doing as soon as the class ends. So much for learning.

Squirming in seats as if they were on anthills. Disrespect afire.

The parent sends his trophy kid to school expecting the school to be a parent.

White kids, black kids… gotta have a cell phone. The parent has allowed texting to replace family. Parents are lazy when it becomes time to say "no". It is a choice that is made by someone. If a parent had no parent, cannot a hero break the cycle? Blame has become the game. Accountability denied.

Fathers have left. Black fathers have left even more. Hey, they were never there at delivery.

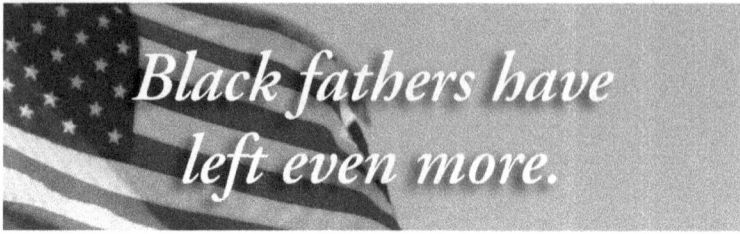

The child enters the classroom without respect. It is a music class. The black music teacher is probably as good as it gets. Though he is still black....

The class is abuzz with itself. He creatively concludes that teaching about Beethoven will not happen seated, for stillness no longer sits. So all are told to lie down on the floor and close their eyes and listen. Guess what? Mission accomplished. All heard a full symphony for the first time.

Parents complained. They did not send their children to school to learn about floors.

But is that not where learning begins?

From the bottom up?

When parents don't parent, teachers can't teach.

No teacher left behind?

Maybe it is time for parents to lie on the floor and listen......

Isn't there music to be heard?

Rap Buds

Ear buds are now the jewelry of the intellect.

All audio consciousness flows through the thin Bluetooth wires into the skulls of the culturally famished. LOL.

Rap is the genre that teaches bad grammar and celebrates indecent imagery...

Where is vocabulary going?

To the streets?

How can one expect to find a job if 50% of one's waking hours are consumed by tunes without redeeming value.

How does a young black male go for an interview when he doesn't own a white shirt or pants that fit? The deck is stacked.

Parents don't want schools to have dress codes. Kids complain. It's always the same. Attitude becomes the uniform. Isn't it time for schools to once again require the uniform... School crest, jackets, ties... oh, what a dream....

How can a teacher teach a mind numbed by incoherent definitions of good behavior?

Why can't we rap about good?

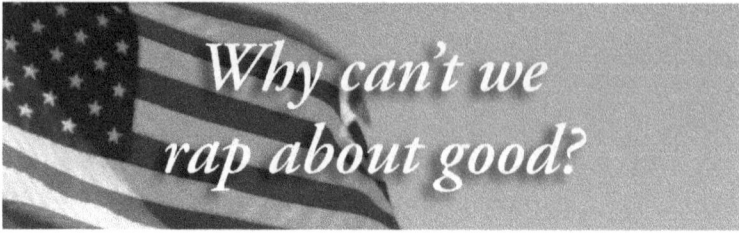

Why is goodness no longer taught? Why is blackness such a yoke...? Did I say joke?

How about some rap that says rap needs to be rapped? RAP. Real Angry People.

When you stick those things in your ears the odds are you are decreasing learning. What a wonderful side-effect.

Ear buds. Hmmm...buds come from seeds that are planted or the beginning of a new spring where blossoms and leaves once again flourish in all their majesty.

Ears will bud if good seeds are planted.

How about seeds talking of the beauty of Truth and values, you know... good things... or how about stories of people helping people?

Once upon a time I got to know BUD/S too. So much pain and endurance was required. So much learning, so much change. Not easy not quitting. But graduating from Basic Underwater Demolition Seal training changed my life. No ear buds there. No garbage in. Just a hard rap on your skull reminding you that being good requires giving; giving it all.

Who makes the money off of rap?

Who tells who what to sing?

Why can't we rap about good?

Bum rap otherwise....

No Color

NO COLOR TV???

NO COLOR?

You mean we have to go back to black and white? Television without color?

What about contrast and high definition? You gotta be kidding!

People with no color on Jeopardy?

Why has color become so important? Why do we actually fight over color? Lives have been lost over color. What in the hell does colored mean anyway? A finished page in a coloring book?

What color is a heart? What color is a bone?

Yet there is not one flower of any color that is not beautiful.

You can say there is not one bird that flies that is not beautiful regardless of color.

There is not one baby that is born that is not beautiful regardless of color.

So how did we let our thinking be colored by color? Why do we

What color is a heart?

have race defined by color. How stupid are we? Really. Are we racing to a finish that will devour us?

Color does only one thing, it enhances beauty. To make it otherwise is a sin. Sheer stupidity. But we have.

March in Selma…. MLK….. Robert Kennedy…. Nelson Mandela….. Abraham Lincoln….. Beauty.

Blackness. Whiteness. Color without color.

Am I getting somewhere with this? It is true that there are more blacks in poverty and without a parent. It is true that the streets have become the universities of anger and entitlement. You can't escape color in this equation. If you are young and black… "You have a problem Houston"….

Maybe we need Victory Gardens where all colors can flourish again. Every seed treated with individual nourishment. Not too much, not too little. Just enough to let it know it can only grow if it accepts the rules and discomfort. Equal opportunity. No seed left behind.

No color. Let's just get it out of the discussion. Surgeons do.

It will require manners, respect, discipline, and love.

Where can you get all this?

There is one place where there is no color.

And it ain't on TV.

Satellite antennas seem to know.....

Privilege White

Your move.

White Knight takes Black Pawn.

Ouch.

Just Kidding.

Draw. Nobody wins. Or everybody wins???

When you are taken do you get kicked off the board??

Life is not a game. And race is not a color. Unless you want to make it so.

Culture? African American, Italian American, French American, Russian American, Hindu American??? French Canadian??? Israeli Arab??? Where does it end?

Are there really any borders any more? Certainly not on the cell phone. Walls are coming down. Old fights are getting old.

The new fights are getting vicious. Religious and political. There is some real evil lurking in the shadows.

White Knight takes Black Pawn.

Oh, what's another beheading???? No game here.

Yet it is still a privilege to be born white. And American. For most this would be their first choice. Life is that way sadly, but a goal should be that it is a privilege to be born anywhere…. i.e. if fair….. But then fair is not reality. Just another distant dream.

How we act is how we define privilege. Do we offer courtesy and respect with colorblind eyes? We should… then we can open them and no longer feel uncomfortable.

We have a racial mess. Like all the pieces are knocked over on the chess board. Kings and Queens are lying in the same fields as the Pawns. Each must offer a hand to the other to pick themselves back up; and without attorneys. Five fingers at a time, black intertwining white. In the streets and in the White House.

Privilege must be defined as the honor to help someone else, anyone else. And without a second thought. "It is my privilege to help you."

In a country with the highest of Declarations there must be an answer to be found. We live on the best chessboard in the world, the United States of America.

It should be a privilege to be Black.

It should be meaningless to be either.

White privilege?

Off with your head.

Trackside

Into the gates.

They're off!!

Galloping furiously into the first turn.

Crowds on the right cheering wildly.

Trackside is so exciting at the Kentucky Derby.

Which side of the track are you on?

One side is mostly white.

The other side of the tracks is different, and poorer... a lot poorer.

Or East St. Louis? Know it?

When one is in the womb there is no knowledge as to which side of the tracks you will take your first breath in. You could be conceived on one side and be born on the other. We get no choice. We don't even get to bet.

Are tracks borders? How easy are they to get across? Sometimes

Which side of the track are you on?

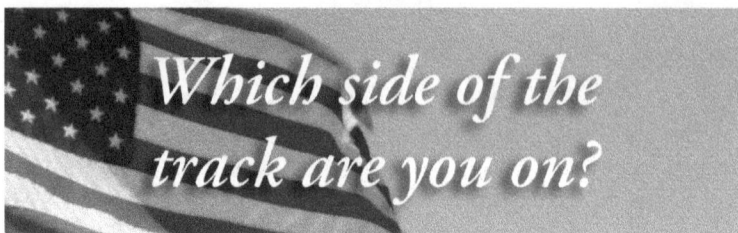

they are muddy. Sometimes they are busy. Sometimes they are dangerous.

The odds are that if you are black the side is already determined. Does a kid ever look across the tracks and wonder? What it is like to be a different color?

My friends have no color. Friends, that's all. No tracks around here.

But there are economic tracks… and there are the streets. Streets have become the tracks that are very difficult to cross. Streets teach anger not reconciliation. Churches have to be gunned down for the tracks to be seen.

The other side of the tracks? Everyone wants to be on the one side. In the grandstands at Churchill Downs. On the right side of the one mile oval. The outside where all the fun is.

We now have new tracks in our homes. Slowly dividing the family into sides. It is no longer about color. It is about cell phone rights. The new oval.

Religion divides. Politics divides. Money divides. Pride divides. Sin divides.

Change the name to Evil Downs.

The new track we are allowing to be built.

Ring tone.

Hear the bugle?

Red White Blue

No black kid left behind?

Go where there is no color.

Start with the United States Military.

Want to get off the streets? Want to see equality?

Do the pushups. Do the Run. Till it ain't fun?

Then you complain of the pain. Then you laugh because it is free.

And so it will be. No color to see.

Enlist and take the journey to the ends of the world. Every port can be seen.

Every city can be felt.

But not if you stay in the street where only mirrors you meet.

Army, Air Force, Marines, Navy, Coast Guard, National Guard.

They're all there, waiting, for you to seek the cure.

Manhood is not found on the street. Duuuhhh..??

Manhood is not found on the street.

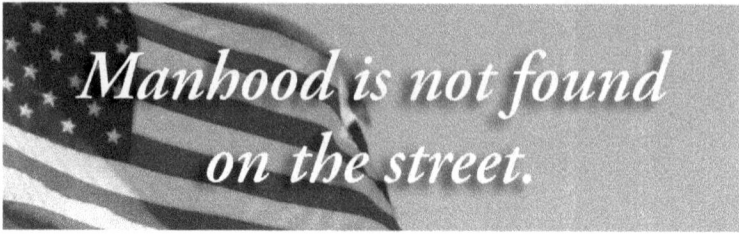

Tattoo all you want. Inside you are still meek.

Somehow the military has been dissed by the left… as if it were evil to protect, to serve, to sacrifice. The system is in place to make men out of boys, so… the streets lose their toys…

Draft our wandering youth.

Teach them manners.

Teach them respect.

Teach them loyalty.

To their family.

And to the old Red, White, and Blue.

Instructor Waddell

I wrote a piece a while ago entitled PDTMWTD… Please Don't Tell Me What To Do.

It was targeted at kids who don't like their parents telling them what to do… Well… and maybe it applies to husbands too??? You get the picture… any of us at any time. PDTMWTD.

When we tell someone what to do we are trying to warn them of possible consequences that we see that we think they don't see.

We all have to learn the same hard way; by experiencing and dealing with our own decisions. We want them to be ours. Why should we trust anyone else's opinion? "Enough with the advice!" we say. Of course, I am still saying that to my wife today….

Then… when we get a job we have to listen to our boss. Groan. If we really grow up we listen to our customers and clients, not ourselves. This is difficult, but it happens because it is paycheck driven. We listen and learn.

So it appears it is the incentive that is important. What is the incentive today when all kids withdraw into the self-assuring world of their cell phone? We are in trouble. They are affirmed

The word "No" is not allowed.

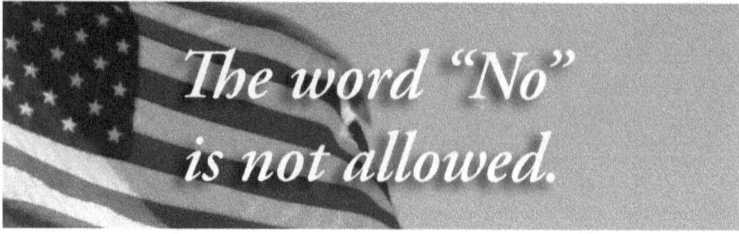

by their insecure social network, not by our wisdom. They no longer "look up" to anything.

The word "No" is not allowed. Children are taught the nuances of "child abuse" and only have to tell their teachers and there will be a knock on the door.

I was blessed with great parents, spankings, and a plethora of "No's". Thank God.

But it was not until the military did I fully begin to appreciate what "No" meant. If you wanted to be a Navy Frogman/ SEAL the INSTRUCTORS were waiting with snarling teeth and monstrous threats of pain. If you did not say "YES INSTRUCTOR" to everything they suggested there was a real price. Too many pushups, too many sit ups, too many pull-ups, too many runs, too many swims... "Are they crazy?" I would think to myself. Is this nonsense really worth it? Why were they so strict? Why was my instructor Bernie Waddell so scary behind his wry smile?

Why??? Because all hell could rain down on you if you showed disrespect in any way, shape, or form. So just do what he asks and get on with your moment. Mile after mile crawling, running, and swimming in the freezing winter during Hell Week weeded out the non-survivors. The Yes Men.

You see... the instructors knew what would happen to you if you were not forged properly. You would be killed when it could have been avoided. Your swim buddy would have been put in peril unnecessarily. The mission aborted because you did not heed your instructor.

We need instructors in order to become all that we have the potential to become. Values must be honed in sweat and pain. We need to learn that freedom is not for free. If you are not conditioned, you will not be strong enough to stand in the winds of life. Laziness destroys potential.

There is white and black, good and evil, yes and no, do's and don'ts....

Values became valuable.

Serving others became more important than serving self.

Prayer became real.

Morality was affirmed.

God Bless You Instructor Bernie Waddell... and Godspeed.

And God Bless all the instructors everywhere.

And parents too.

Instructor Waddell was black.

Grand Theft Ought To

The biggest theft going on today is our kids.

We are looking the other way as they are jammed into a car that goes nowhere.

They are the victims of wanting to be happy in the instant.

The "Whatever" children going wherever there are smiles.

Their sundaes are drugs.

On Sundays.

We ought to do something about it but all we do is legalize it. Hard drugs flow across our borders like salmon up the streams.

A kid on drugs goes nowhere and becomes eligible for nothing. A parent who does nothing is a de-facto drug dealer. Hey, that is parenting!

It is we who create the demand and satiate the immediate need.

It is all about unspoken loneliness and lack of social consciousness.

Let's get off our asses America.

It is the cancer of the poor and the poor in heart, who happen to be rich.

Hello nation, you are the laughing stock of the enemy. You do not take the well-being of your children seriously. What future is there for the enabled? For the "No Worries" generation.

There is a real war looming on the horizon in… let's say for kicks… the Middle East… They are promising recognition and dignity to their warrior… to our lost youth.

How in the world can we help our double dis-affected black youth? Gotta start somewhere, so let's look it square in the face.

Not another debate in Washington on the "Ought To Amendment." Give a searing mandate to the states to test in schools, to create dress codes, to meet out punishment like 50 years ago. Get the unions out of our children's lives. Out of our teacher's lives. Teach values, teach the horror of drugs. Teach the evil of pride. Teach the beauty of helping someone get off drugs…. And off the street.

For once do the black kids first and watch the whites follow. Now that is a halleluiah!!

A spade is a spade and a spade is black.

Deal them a Royal Spade Flush.

Let's get off our asses America.

WWIII is within our borders.

Truth or Consequences

Truth or Consequences, New Mexico.

Maybe 8,000 people. Less than 1% black.

Got hot springs and a post office.

Was named after a TV show of the 50's.

You had to tell the truth or face the consequences.

We no longer tell the truth nor face any consequences as our feelings are protected by the law.

There just has to be consequences! "No Worries" should be redacted from vocabularies. We need more worries to control behavior.

There sure are consequences in the military. Come on guys... show some spine...

I think the discussion really should be about Love or Consequences. Not love of drugs or rap, but of Love of fellow man, friend, and family.

Truth or Consequences, New Mexico.

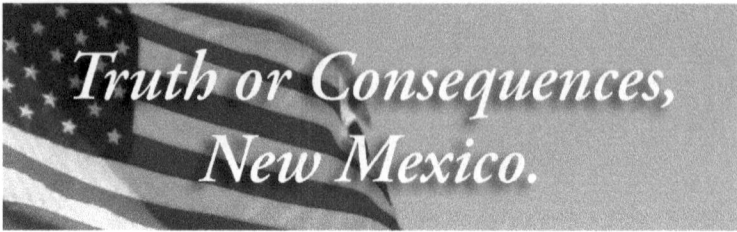

The people you should admire are those who have helped others…who have shown uncomplicated Love.

Love is Truth. Think about it. Really.

Your first love is your first exposure to Truth. The feeling is so honest and compelling. Pure. You just want to help this other person. Pure. It is Truth.

As the years pass it gets diluted and we lose the Truth. Again and again, the time you feel most true is when you do something unselfish for another. The definition of love. There is no room for color. Unselfishness is power. Unselfishness is good.

Our entire life is just a search for Truth. Truth un-complicates things. Unselfishness un-complicates things. In a love of Truth you are set free to make a difference. The consequences are astounding as people silently applaud you.

Recognition is what so many pursue in the Mean Streets and in the Wall Streets.

The consequences are always disappointment and lives squandered.

No black life should be squandered any longer.

Black pigment is made up of all colors.

Solve its problem and you bring all colors to life and Truth.

Truth is Love.

You can't Cross that one out.

West Point

West of what?

What is the point?

Forty miles north of New York City.

Founded by Thomas Jefferson in 1802.

And there is gold in them 'thar hills.

16,000 acres.

Black Gold. The colors of the United States Military Academy.

Except there is more to the story. Regardless of color you can graduate from West Point as a Second Lieutenant with lives soon to be in your hands. You had to work hard to get there and… be approved. Your speech, bearing, attitude, and accomplishments are taken into consideration. You see, you have to be able to communicate clearly and effectively to protect your men in battle. Big time responsibility. Duuuhh…?

Black Gold. Colors yes…. But black kids can go there and become leaders! They are mining black gold. Our black kids are the

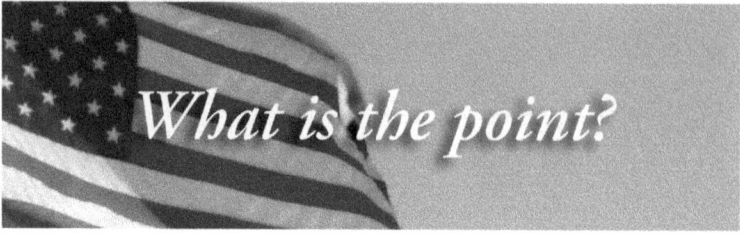

untapped gold veins in our country. Lost in the deep dark mines of the streets and broken homes. Born into chaos.

West Point and all the military welcomes regardless of race. You just have to stop with the shit and get your act together. Take advice and respect family and authority and values. Tough assignment?? Too bad.

But we have such a blessing here guys. You are a great natural resource. Escape from the streets and the evil that is keeping you from being somebody. Right here in our own back yard! This is where you are treated like gold and brought to a beautiful pure luster. The polishing can be uncomfortable. You have to learn to run and do pushups….. Hey, the girls will think you are a god. It is so worth it.

Black and Gold.

Black is our Gold.

The President should be challenging all of you to join.

OK… African American gold.

Hello?

Rules Say

The rules say.

Obey me.

The fine print.

The print is fine.

So before any action can be taken, a full review of the rules, aka, the fine print too, must be taken. Appropriate response levels must be assigned. Punishments detailed.

More rules too often slow down response and decision making. If somebody hits my sister, I have no time for rules. My fist is the rule.

We have become a society afraid of the rules. We debate and argue endlessly as to the rightness of every rule. You need an attorney always with you. Try and buy a dishwasher from Lowes or Home Depot and the fine print you are expected to sign is indecipherable.

In schools the Principal is afraid of the school board, the teacher of the principal, the principal of the union, the student of the

Let decisions fly free again.

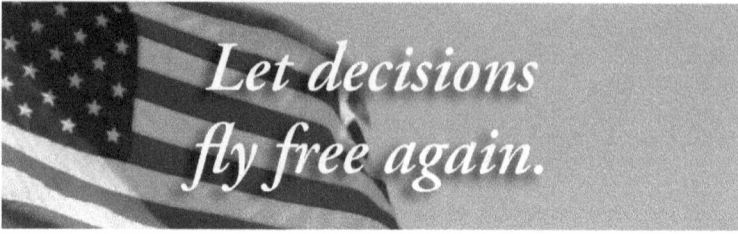

teacher, the parent of the teacher, the student of whatever and all ever.

The bureaucracy of permission is sand in the transmission. We are stifling our identity.

Values have been dismissed from the classroom. Yet it is values that makes order out of chaos. But in the classroom you can't say what is 'right' as it is preaching from a wing. LOL. Godless topics are the only ones universally approved. Isn't this a crock of shit?

Now… you insert the black kid with his expectations and loss thereof and we have race muddying up the equation.

We have to return to teaching values. Let the teacher guide his class. Stop the excessive reporting and tattling and trust them to care. The classroom cannot be run by the Principal or the union… or the parent…

The parent has to be admonished for sending their undisciplined offspring to the school. They want the teacher to make up for their lack of effort and resolve. They want more rules to solve what they did wrong. Phooey.

Grow up School Board, Principal, Teacher, Union, Parent, and Student…

Trust the teacher. Teach trust. Live trust. Trust values.

Let decisions fly free again.

There is something corrupt going on...

And the 'Rules Say".....?

Whatever.

Black Box

A black box is often a coffin.

Except that now you can have them in any color.

Even rainbow.

We continue to look for answers that evade us...

Like in all the wrong places.

When there is a bad accident we look for the answers in the black boxes.

Soon black boxes will be going into cars and whatever else.

Body cameras are kind of black boxes... don't you think?

We want answers and we want them now. Maybe we should surgically implant micro black boxes in our kids to find the answers as to why they are so rude and disrespectful... Why they do drugs and waste their potentials. We need something to blame it on other than ourselves.

We too always have our cell phones in hand...

Role models??

A black box is often a coffin.

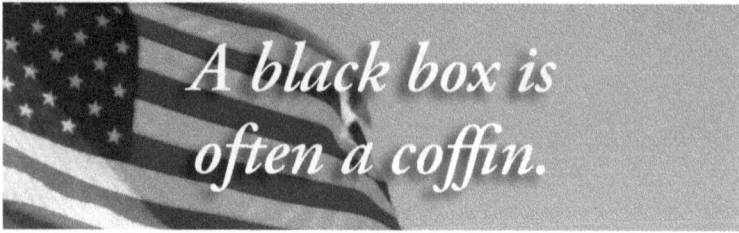

Maybe we need black boxes in schools and classrooms... Maybe it is essential to have body cameras on teachers so we can believe what they have to deal with. So parents can see how they have failed.

Are black people in a black box? I think so. Who made it?

This box has to be disassembled and we have to do it. All the sides of the box have to be defined, addressed, and disposed of. All 4 sides and the top and bottom.

1. Ignorance – Work hard in school – Leave the streets – Acknowledge evil.

2. Bad attitudes – Need fathers to come back.

3. Disrespect - Respect authority and family.

4. Discipline - There must be real consequences.

5. Integrity - Live in Truth & humility.

6. Compassion – Judging wisely with patience.

You can make up your own, but the black family is in trouble... (Not that the white family isn't.).

The black family is strong when they are part of a dynamic

church family. Values are still taught in churches. Shame on us they aren't in schools. Only sensitivity to sensitivities is taught there.

Our white schools are black boxes. Funny.

The teacher is no longer respected as the independent incubator of success. Classrooms are now just repositories of fine print, infinite rules, and instructions. Where the bully's feelings are as important as the victim's. Huuuhh? Sympathy to evil…?? And values now taught as bigotry… Huuuhh? Black box or empty box?

If someone hits my kid, I say hit back harder regardless.

No consequences and you create PHD's in entitlement.

Yes, the answers are found in black boxes.

Schools are black boxes even if they are white on the outside…

I have seen a lot of black coffins that look real good lined in white…

Now a black and white milkshake is real sweet…

Let's mix it up gang.....

Smiley Face

We all know a smiley face is a sign of happy.

We love it as it kinda makes you smile for a micro-second... inside...

They have white teeth too.

But in some you can't see the teeth. Does that mean they are black?

I wonder what white folk would look like with black teeth.

Smiles can be evil, but for the most part they make you comfortable about another person. A lot of successful people are blessed with a constant smile. A twinkle in the eye... and a "nice to see you" kind of look.

White teeth sure helps. Today the vain sport is fake teeth, enameled super white. It is funny to see the newscasters on TV with great front teeth but the back ones are regular kinda yellow. Funny.

Black people are born with white teeth and white bones and red

They have white teeth too.

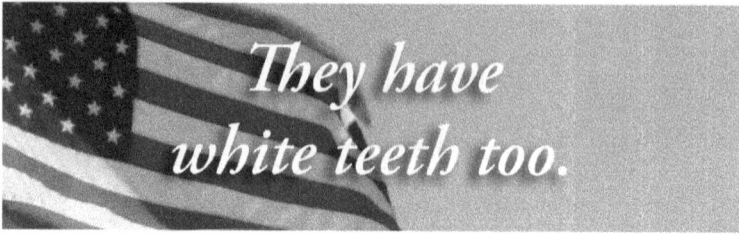

blood. But we act like they are so different because they are so easy to label and identify from color of skin.

I love toast. Pure Wonder Bread in a toaster turns brown to get it to the rich hot texture to take butter perfectly. It is still the same inside.

When you smile you reveal who you really are... Fake smiles are so fake and we all know it. Real smiles with real white teeth means the person must be just like me.

People are just people, regardless of the continent they live on or came from.

It is how we behave that changes the equation.

Lack of education makes things hard for one.

No stable family makes things hard for one.

Missing parents means love cannot be taught properly.

Dismissiveness of values is cancerous.

The marginalization of church is a last straw.

Rationalizing evil is the final surgery.

Has liberal education liberated the inane?

You might as well have black teeth as nothing more will matter.

The only icon left on the cell phone selfie will be the "Scowly Face".

AAT

AAT sounds like where we are at.

Emphasized with an extra A.

Where are we at?

The world is on the brink again.

The brink of war and more fleeing refugees.

What happens to an economy inundated with a 100,000 homeless or more?

We are on the brink of our family being destroyed....

Brinkmanship... Ha!

We are less in control of evil than ever.

The digital age has given us freedoms we cannot control.

We race to understand and label all that is happening.

Trying to understand that the genie is out of the box.....

Where does a kid find out what is really true?

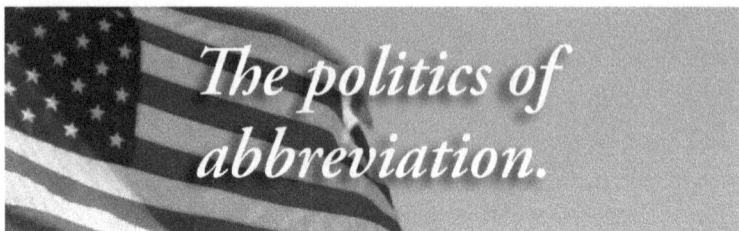

The politics of abbreviation.

Where is meaningful hope found?

BSA, AARP, FBI, CIA, DOT, TSA, USA, AAA, KKK, BFF.......

All of these define attempts to make a difference of some sort.

It has gotten so bad that my friend seriously refers to himself as an AAT. "Any Awful Thing"?... no... it stands for "African American Teacher". That is how he reaches out... no longer just a teacher. He is an AAT... not even in Wikipedia yet...

Labels and abbreviations provide security to bureaucracies. They create their own languages.

The politics of abbreviation. The clubs of the protected.

So all you AATs... how is it going?

Let's make an AAT blazer crest. Khaki pants, white shirt and crest tie.

Gucci loafers.

Rock N Roll

Race music... It was called... or rhythm and blues. In the '50s.

Chuck Berry... 45 rpm records... and the independence began.

Chuck was black and the whites ate it up. Color began to roll.

The rock of racism was forever changed.

All around the world the youth were dancing with a new rebellious beat.

Music became the international equalizer.

Somehow music penetrates the walls of totalitarianism and injustice.

Today the internet and Wi-Fi and Bluetooth send the frequencies of the spirit everywhere.

Some lyrics are beautiful testimonies to love and truth that we can privately embrace with affirming emotion. Yet, great numbers speak of disrespect and evil... glorifying them...

I wonder why those who are destroying our values and morals don't "get it". They are leaving a heritage of shame and

Long live Rock n Roll.

destruction... subtle... but devastating; especially devastating to the family. Respect abandoned.

The poor are being taught entitlement. The black, hate. The white, laziness.

Or any combination thereof.

Yet go into a church and hear the soaring songs of Hope and Truth. Redeeming and powerful for those who show the courage to enter those doors. Halleluiah... (had to say it...)

Rock n Roll. Kids still use the term. Did Rock start things to Roll? The questioning spirit that is at the heart of all music since. Leaping over borders with internet blazing speed. It is hard to censor music... "Thinking" is on a roll. Concerts still bring enormous crowds of the searching young.

Musicians have an enormous responsibility if they "get it". They can shape minds. They can make doing good necessary. They can make loving and helping others symphonies of unselfishness and humility. They can make "doing good" sexy. Poets can.

Evil, greed, pride, self-indulgence, and vanity can be marginalized. Studios have to stop being greedy and feeding evil. These captains of Rock need to be able to look their grandchildren in the eye and know they have set a good example. That they have the courage to be real men. To be champions of values.

Long live Rock n Roll.

Let the new bass lines guide our feet back to the Rock.

Thank you Chuck Berry.

Deep Blues

I had mentioned in an earlier book a first year in the Navy spent aboard an oceanographic research vessel, USS Marysville, EPCER 857 out of Point Loma, San Diego, Naval Electronics Laboratory.

We cruised at 6 miles an hour from San Francisco to Acapulco. We collected marine organisms and measured temperature versus depth. They wanted to know as much as they could about the ocean for submarines.

Especially the depths at which thermoclines formed. Radical temperature shifts that created a wall that submarines could hide beneath. Their secrecy of movement was very, very important to survival and their secret activities.

Down that deep, the ocean is black. There is no light... other than what is inside the submarine. Pitch black otherwise. But black and white sailors knowing no color, willing to sacrifice for one another. Amazing... Imagine all that activity going on in a giant nuclear submarine and it doesn't exist.

As I have gotten deeper and deeper into the feelings and insights

Down that deep the ocean is black.

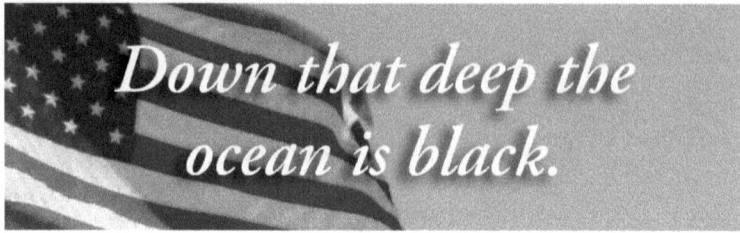

of my black teacher friend... my AAT friend... I have started to liken it to this submarine. Many secrets and hidden powers deep within. In fact most all black people have an emotional thermocline that they hide their real feelings beneath.

All-day, every day they sense out of the corners of their eyes and ears subtle references that signal cloaked racism or its residual. Maybe like a woman walking through a parking lot pretending she is not looking. To... avoid danger...

There are so many cues that the black person can see that we can't. We have no clue what we radiate to them... up in the warm water.... The subtle discomfort of a white in the presence of a black... or just holding different aspirations due to reality.

So much to envision. My AAT friend is writing his book. All lies therein.

So deep inside the black person are the blues of past hurt and diminished future expectation.

So much has been done to date by so many, Presidents and people.... but more must be achieved. That lies very deep within every black person.

I am hoping that social media will be the final equalizer.

Can it lead us to a new social equality?

Deep blues.

Go there and hear them.

Double Bypass

No, this is not changing lanes or going under two bridges.

Nor is it going around your boss to his boss.

It is emergency surgery to circumvent bad arteries. It is serious stuff. They literally break your breastbone so they can get their hands on your heart and work on the plumbing. I can show you my scar. Oh they threw in a pacemaker as a bonus to keep my heart on the beat. They say the battery lasts 15 years. I am thinking of getting a baseball cap with solar cells on the brim…

They lay these white cloths around the entry, with spreaders holding things back. All they see is red and some white bone….

We all are going to die. For some, open heart surgery gives you some additional years.

Does our nation need open heart surgery? Where is its heart by the way? Are we talking about downsizing bureaucracy and entitlement?

Or are we talking about the cancer of hidden racism lingering in our arteries?

Set teachers free.

Does a black man's heart look different than a white man's heart? The surgeon can't tell the difference. Now I tan pretty dark......

Somewhere inside the heart is the soul... or whatever you want to call the essence of an individual... from birth... Souls have all the potential in the world. Life circumstance and love molds it into a good heart or a cold one... Like hearts, souls all look alike too.

Well, you have to believe in something rather than nothing.

Your choice.

We need to dig deep into our hearts and say out loud again "all men are created equal".

We all need to be white surgeons and work on our own hearts. It is our hearts that can change all. Our hearts are capable of doing a double bypass on lingering racism.

Let go of the past.

Get religion's values back in the classrooms.

Set teachers free.

To teach the difference between good and evil.

Stop the political correctness syndrome.

It hides the Truth.

One red heart at a time we must bypass the urge to judge by race.

And pace our Maker.

Union Pacific

In the dining cars with the great windows and white linen tablecloths were the poised and dignified black stewards.

Yes Ma'am. Yes Sir.

The best were assigned to the private cars.

Building the railroads required hard work by many races, mixing sweat and tears as the heavy ties were placed and the steel rails laid. From coast to coast. Magnificent transportation of muscle and resolve. Bodies and souls a testimony to accomplishment at any price....

Brotherhoods became unions to fight for the rights of those who did the sweating. Dues and promises and threats were formalized. In the beginnings they were noble and effective as workers acquired new rights.

But somewhere along our way the union has become powerful and bureaucratic and political. The individual worker became a statistic. Decision making now has to travel up through many levels. Supervisor to his supervisor to his supervisor.... Little is left to supervise save some final detached and political decision.

Yes Ma'am. Yes Sir.

Union decisions affect most all business save for the small ones who can stay under the radar. Benefits promised or coerced. Profits and revenue streams that are self-justifying… Kinda. Teacher unions starting pure and becoming porridges of political correctness. Tenure-driven dishonesty.

Teachers are supposed to be the bastions of idealism, integrity, and character. Yet every teacher has to defer to his boss. No one confronts anyone. Behind closed doors judgements are delivered without defense.

I thought principals were the protectors of fairness. Champions of values and Truth. Not guardians of mistakes… Nor stewards of spills.

Union Pacific.

A grand railroad still serving her country.

I think there are more white stewards now. Must be progress. Need a count.

Pacify the Union with fairness and compassion.

Love hurts, when it is honest.

BTSD

Black Traumatic Stress Disorder.

Hold on to your seats if you think this is racist.

Because it isn't

Hey there isn't anything tough that happens to someone that doesn't cause some kind of stress disorder. What about divorce?? On the kids?? Or the father leaving when the kids are young? Much less any violence in life...

Even Executive Orders cause disorder.

But if you are a young black kid with untouched dreams and a naïve, thirsty brain what you are going to take in is a shock. It will require internalized decisions about the outside world. You will have new antenna to sense what others don't have to.

Check the race box on any form and you are classified as different. Any remark about Negroes will be picked up and filed. The white kid has less to concern himself with... Much less.

The poor level of black education and the enormous unemployment rate of young male blacks are cauldrons of stress.

Even Executive Orders cause disorder.

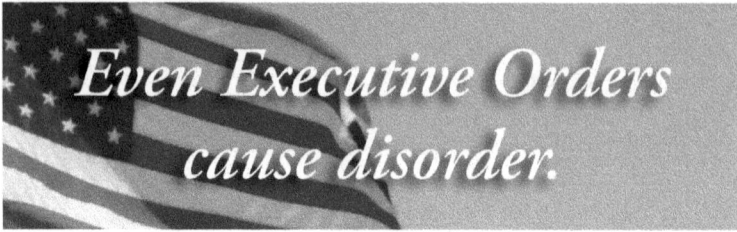

Energy that does not erupt in positive activity. Maybe it is time to get a Job Corps formed as an option to the military. "Put us to work" should be the cry.

BTSD cannot be cured with therapy and counseling. Work can provide accountability structure and attitude adjustment. A sense of self making a contribution is essential to healing. Singing on Sunday also has meaning to those who have the courage to walk inside….. Nothing finer than to hear in Carolina in the morning a crowd raised "Halleluiah". Can't hurt no one and sure puts a smile on all but the terminally ill. LOL.

Black pride is great, but not if it separates. Real pride can only come when respect is earned and when whites find the humility of equality. Whites have to dig deeper and see the pain. Blacks have to look in the mirror and find respect… self-first then to all others once outside. Manners and respect are essential to cure the disorder. Both sides have to man up, bite the bullet, and look deep into their brother's eyes.

The slightest hint of racial bias is always felt. Duuuhhh?? We must stop pretending it isn't noticed.

You know how your ears pick up when anyone is talking about you?

Aren't we sensitive to every opinion of ourselves?

Criticism hurts... until one turns it into a positive.

BTSD

Better Try Seeing Differently.

Reverse Racism

Goes around, comes around...

Slavery. Religion. Wealth. Poverty. Democracy. Socialism. Communism.

Materialism. Informationalism.

In our lives we have seen societies stand still, cultures regress, and justice debated... or some would say deleted...

We killed Martin Luther King. Oops... Don't go there...
We, meaning a culture that had not been able to find values universal enough to create barriers to evil and prejudice. We have proceeded down a road where everything that was black or white has become a new shade of grey. Laws were established that try to blind one to race rather than embrace it. Subtle, but just as dangerous.

Think about it.

Religion has been morphed into an avoidance category. Wealth and poverty are now both evil. Democracy bows her noble knee to lesser. Socialism and Communism are failures for the people. Materialism is celebrated as it strips the soul of worth.

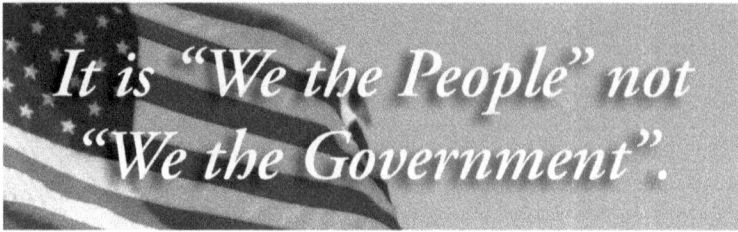

It is "We the People" not "We the Government".

And lastly, the new "Informationalism" is our last hope. With the god of Google we hopefully have all the facts. All the facts, past and present!!! Truth. Truth sought since Biblical times. Truth at last. Thank God almighty Truth at last...

Okay, with media and educators alike having equal access to truth how are we doing??? We have spy satellites and information gathering capabilities beyond imagination. We are all in data mines. You could say our identities are slaves to the data mining industry... Interesting twist??? It's okay with me as I no longer have anything to hide anyway...

Are we better off? Are we doing better???

As we ponder the polls and data of politics we see enormous demographic evolutions in America. Ethnic minorities are becoming the new majorities. People of color are getting their own languages legalized. When was the last time you saw a warranty in English only? Race boxes on forms are increasing. You can't say white... it's Caucasian... Who ever heard of Caucasian??? I am finally insecure about saying white. What do I say? And ... I am becoming the new minority.

Goes around, comes around....

But for sure I am an American, the land of immigrants and

opportunity. So is it time to take the race check boxes off all forms??? Reverse discrimination is growing. Now that profiling is such a bad process, what are we left with? What can we base judgments on? Better get a lawyer, the new god of truth. Make sure you have been read your "Informationalism Rights".

As I write this I wonder where it will all lead. In the best country in the world we have raised disagreement to new heights. Our political parties should be ashamed of not being able to raise the dignity of their process. Self-interest pervades decision making.

I like the most recent quote by someone. It is "We the People" not "We the Government".

Until we the people re-find our common values based on our Judeo-Christian heritage I fear that this white old man will die with a tear on his cheek.

Color TV

Color TV.

That is when it all started.

Sometime in the 60's.

Before then everything was simple.

Everybody knew what they were supposed to do.

Manners mattered.

Black and white were the only colors on the original 9" TV screen. The whole family huddled around. They were together. Laughing at the same time, young and old. Most today have no clue how much better life was in so many ways. I think we forget about history in the rush to immediacy. Sad.

Penguins are black and white. They have good lives except for the sharks. Our society was black and white with nothing in between. Morality was more black and white. Rules and laws were black and white. They just needed to mature so the white would show more respect to the black. Tough journey.

Color changed everything. You could see the shades of difference

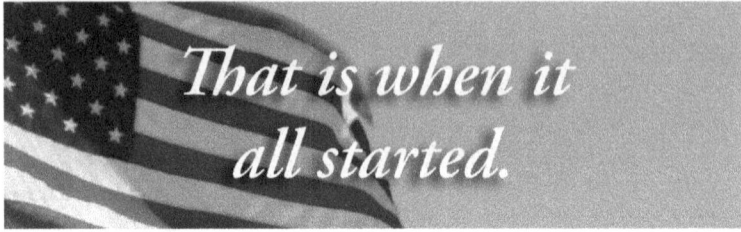

between white and black. The inside started to matter more. Wonder what a penguin looks like inside? LOL.

Color TV screens have become so large, like 6 feet diagonal, that reality can be confused with the screen. And as that happens we become lost in a surreal reality and it modifies our thinking and understanding of what is real. So much time is spent looking at television that the world outside has little time to form us other than when tragedies happen.

Nothing to laugh about?

Now we have micro color TV screens on our cell phones.

Television has given us a lot to think about when we are not busy watching it.

No time for a sunset when texting.

No time for the hungry puppy when texting.

Texting in the bathroom is the new privacy. LOL.

Black Hole

I can't see the bottom!

How deep is it?

How far down do I have to go?

Can I take a light with me?

It is so dark and scary.

You go first.

Is it in a cave? Or on the ocean floor where it is dark already. Is it in a mine or is it below a large grating underground? If it just wasn't so black down there….

In outer space are the largest black holes of all where scientists say there is nothing. Yet those black holes consume galaxies and stars. Creating a black density that defies logic. Well… at least street logic.

In either case, what is unimaginable is horrific. Where nothing exists?

How far down do I have to go?

Actually, black is made up of all colors. We all become one color? Maybe black?

So what is all the fuss? Let's take color out of the equation and let's take religion out, and let's take histories out. Oh, and lastly, let's just take labels out... Of our clothes too.

Let's just be people. Good and bad.

The good people can fight the bad. Let's hope the former win.

I'd rather be with the good people. What does it take to join? Are there more good people than bad? Usually numbers matter.....

I hear that most quit trying to be a good person worthy of the Good People Army, GPA.

The secret is to be a good person day by day, one day at a time... just giving it all to your instructors who you have to trust. Like in Hell Week in the SEALs... Life was never meant to be easy...

Look around and under the surface of all you know. There are some tough struggles going on. Children who are lost in attitude. Adults unhappy with income, station, or relationships..... So caught up in self that they can't become truly good.

Truly good means thinking of others first. Getting out of yourself makes you gooder.

You are in a black hole until then…..

To get to the outer reaches of the universe it takes a long time with even the best spacecraft… if ever.

But we all gotta try.

Not the Orion, but the USS Faith.

Never quit and black will be white.

Tar Baby

Once upon a time there was a person named us.

We were at the age where we were desperately looking for answers but didn't know the questions.

Nowhere to turn but to our peers, who provided us the comfort of their ignorance. LOL.

We grew up, emboldened in our image, pride, and ego… and accomplished much. Had possessions, and friends, and acceptance in our groups of friends. The wine was good.

Then we had kids. They had lots of questions. They had lots of opinions. They had thoughts that we had never heard of or maybe had? Hormonal hockey came into play. LOL. Mothers screamed. Fathers, when around, said "calm down."

Easy answers were sought by all.

I call the easy answers the tar babies of life.

Something was trying to get us lured into and captured in the tar pit of life. Once you get stuck there it is hard to get out. Very hard. Ask the addict. Ask the person who has it all and is in their

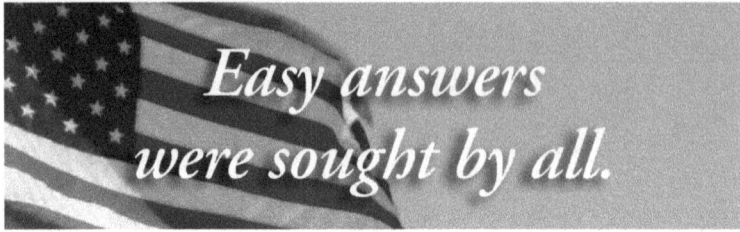

own tar pit. There is hell on earth. It's black and sticky. It's also known as self. You see we get stuck on ourselves and/or stuck in our self. Easy to laugh at until you see that it might be true.

If we want to avoid this trap there is one word which holds a key. It is the "NO" word. If parents don't teach their kids what "No" means then all is lost to the self. Families never form. Love is held at bay. Saying "No" takes courage. It takes leadership. It is essential to survival.

I saw a clip on TV of inner-city kids in a military style boot camp. For the first time they had the word "No" drilled into them. AKA "No" cell phones.... They had never been happier. They had never felt pride before. They were given the tools to climb out of their tar pit.

Respect and values come next. You will never go back once you find them.

Making others more important than self closes the deal and the tar pit is never to be found again.

A tar baby lures others into their pit.

Tar babies like company.

Don't let them stick to you.

Say "No, I choose to grow!"

They will say you are hurting their feelings.

Too bad. Too bad.

White Bread

This is not funny.

White bread is not funny.

White flour is not funny.

My doctor says to avoid it.

So does my wife.

But it is in everything.

In fact, am told anything that is white is not good for me.

What about up in the clouds?

Black Tennis Balls

This ain't about Aunt Jemima... so drop your prejudging now.

This also isn't really about tennis balls.

Nor the USTA...

It ain't about color either...

First of all, in the interests of equal rights and equal insensitivity we will state that in the dark you cannot hit a black tennis ball. Actually in the dark you can't hit a white or yellow one either. Now if you turn the light up a little, the black balls still are elusive. Try to serve as you toss the ball into the sky and it disappears then lands on your head!!

Throw a black ball into the mud and you can't find it.

Police wear black uniforms. Does that make them bad? No, they try hard to keep us all safe. So black is a color of good sometime.

We also have people running around in white robes saying we are evil. Yes, you and I are evil because we live in an evil nation. We don't get it. If someone thinks you are evil, misery is headed your way.

The color of your tennis balls becomes unimportant. You could be found in a gutter with your can unopened. Maybe they opened it and the balls were black. ISIS Tennis anyone?

There are games you don't want to play.

We are playing games with fire.

We are playing games with what we used to believe in.

We are playing games by not forcing solutions.

We are playing games by being partisan.

We are playing games by not saying "No".

We are playing games with self.

We are playing games with religion.

We are playing games with love.

We are playing games with death.

We are playing games with black tennis balls.

Blackface

Al Jolson did not look natural with black makeup back in the black and white film era.

He was called The World's Greatest Entertainer.

His singing had its own style.

It was good entertainment, but what right does a white man have to portray a black person?

Black makeup covering the obvious Caucasian. The black man had suffered enough. Yet, the white man had suffered enough when he left Europe... Who has not suffered?

Suffering is evil. It is not good. It can make you stronger. But we all envision a world without suffering where fairness and justice rule. Compassion and Truth reside in a good society. And Truth is determined by goodness and kindness and love, not by edict and discrimination. Faces must be free of concealment and arrogance.

Our faces are meant to entertain, to show love and happiness and sorrow and hope. How can every face be so unique? Like the stars in the heavens. None should ever be hidden. Only evil hides... until it commits its desecrations...

Suffering is evil.

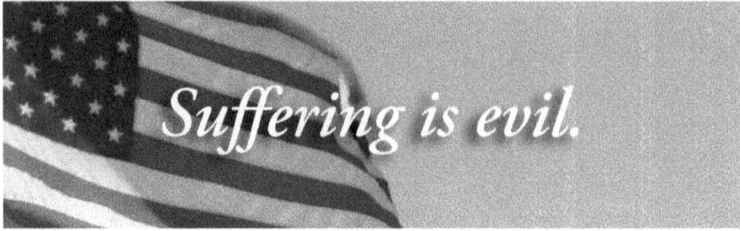

The face of evil hides behind many makeups. It can hide in religion and in government. People make evil happen. Some can be smiling while planning death. Evil is not a debate in a classroom. It beheads good when we look away.

Evil makes women slaves of involuntary sex. Evil dehumanizes mankind. Evil destroys a child in the womb. Evil makes a child fatherless.

Evil is real, not an imagined enemy.

It only yields in the face of great force.

Atomic?

If we don't declare war will we skirmish ourselves to death?

We can only be great if united.

Black and white we must fight.

Singing "Mammy".

Stupid Teacher

How stupid can a teacher be?

Why would you appoint someone to be a teacher if he were stupid?

That would make you stupid.

In the old days teachers were smart. They had real degrees and real experience.

There were rules in the classrooms. You listened.

Today the committees, meetings, reports, and assessments make the front line teacher an administrator. Political correctness for every form and every answer. The only real grade becomes how it reads on the political correctness scale.

The classroom is like the Middle East, hidden battlefields everywhere. Parent organizations, teachers unions, principal's principals. Sponsor interests....

IED. Improvised Educational Devices. Wary be the teacher who steps on one.

Some are white, some are black.

How stupid can a teacher be?

Maybe the teacher is only as stupid as his students.

Students with attitude and no learned respect are really stupid. Because they are dumbing down their futures. They are the bullies of fairness and equality as they deny their classmates focus.

Schools have become so paranoid to sensitivity that they destruct needed values. Professors in universities are becoming liberal gods of nothingness. It takes courage to go against the flow and where nobody wants to go.

Take the handcuffs off the stupid teachers and you may find a raging bull of genius. Tied up for too long. Pamplona in the classroom.

Mothers are teachers. They know what is best for their kids. What good does it do when they say "no" and the classroom says "yes"? What good does it do when they say "study" and the recess crowds say "whatever"?

The smart teacher says give us back our schools. The courageous will give up tenure to be free in the classroom. Unshackle me from the unions so I can stand on my own. Those who study hard will get good grades. Those who don't won't. New intolerance must emerge. It will be a 180, but will thwart failure.

Intolerance of attitude, sloppiness, rudeness, disrespect, bad language, bad dress codes, and…. Must be the siren from the office of the principal.

Call the fire department, our kids futures are burning.

Smart teachers are firefighters.

Beige Love

So she married a Jamaican.

So?

Does a happy 3-year old laugh?

Ask questions?

Care about adult problems?

Of course not. We all know that. We have all been there.

Does a first parental argument scare us?? You bet.

Does seeing mom and dad hold each other and laugh seem right?

Black love. White love. Beige love. Yellow love. Purple love.

Does color really matter? No, except for when we see people as black and white... Then it divides.

However, good and evil must be black and white. Unless... we want to continue down the slippery slope of extinction... "Values" is not a politically correct word any more. Hello?

You can be from any country and marry anyone from any country.

So she married a Jamaican.

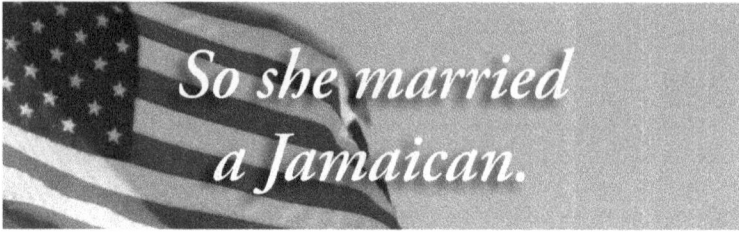

Children will be so mixed that color will disappear if we don't insist on checking the box of black or white....

Children love Love because they love what is good and unselfish. They know what a good deed is or what is scary. They are molded by love or the lack thereof.

Big question. Who taught us Love?

Why do you close your eyes when you kiss? Does everything turn black except for a flash of white excitement?

In Italy the Tuscan palette is many beiges. It is exciting over there. The Italians love life, wine, love, and beige.

Over here we have beat beige to death.

HGTV looks so exciting because of the lack of beige.

Pioneering heroes explore the unknown and take risks. New land where new worlds and cities can emerge.

So a white girl and a Jamaican marry.

Their boys are the new normal.

The only important thing is what they are taught.

Respect for work and others, manners, and how to love.

Helping others is the love needed to pioneer peace.

Pride follows.

Black Anchor

I don't know how many of you have been aboard old ships. But the anchors were all black.

I think they put tar on them to keep them from rusting or something.

Anchors are meant to keep a ship safe... from drifting and from moving in rough weather.

They are heavy with big heavy link chains attached to heavy posts on the ship.

The life of the crew depends on the anchor.

Anchors go down into the deep where color turns black.

A white anchor recently broke from its mooring due to a weak link. That link was truth. For exaggeration turned into a lie. The Truth links were separated and the network floundered. After long meetings in the white officers mess (dining room) the captain announced that they would try a black anchor. You sensed a studied reluctance.

Each day they paused and assured themselves they were not

But the anchors were all black.

taking a risk. Damn, if the new anchor only shined and shined. No longer shoes, but the nation. How can a black man be so elegant and comfortable to receive the world's news from??

Is this not a milestone?

Trust again from media?

Clone this guy.

Make him into all colors for every country.

Go Lester Go.

Rainbow

I wonder if all rainbows are the same.

Can the refraction under a certain circumstance create a blue rainbow?

Oh, I guess you wouldn't see it against the blue sky.

Would the pot of gold be blue?

All we really care about is the pot of gold anyway. We really don't care if the rainbow is red, blue, green, yellow, or whatever. We just go for the gold.

We are colorblind when it comes to money.

We don't care about the color of the drug dealer.

We don't care about the color of the Love dealer.

We all want to be a rainbow and bring happiness to someone, hopefully other than our self. When we put self at the end of the rainbow we cause self-destruction and evil. Evil people put little value on Truth, Peace, or Love. If we can catch them we put them in cells where they cannot see rainbows, until they can.

There is another Rainbow that we try so hard to avoid. We don't

want others to look deep inside us and see what we really are. "I'm just fine" and they go away.

That Rainbow is Prayer. Prayer is not hope. Prayer is asking God to hear your concern. Prayer is humbling yourself. Prayer is admitting there must be something greater than you. Prayer requires the tear of honesty.

Most choose not to go to prayer as they think they still have the answers. Their ego is king and the royalty to be protected. This throne must come down for the ego to be human and meaningful. To be remembered as having done good.

This is the pot of gold at the end of the Prayer Rainbow.

Pray for someone and you can look them in the eye and wink silently at yourself.

It feels good.

It is good.

Be a Rainbow.

Thar's gold in 'dem 'der hills.....

Your Story

Hey kids... when you get older... aka really old... your life begins to make sense.

You can be honest with yourself and know what was good and what was bad.

What bad was done to you and what bad you may have done to others.

More importantly you look at the good others did to you and the good you did to others.

There may be people who will never like you, but what counts is if you have done more good than bad and admit it.

Your story is like no other story ever in the history of existence. More unique than the furthest star in the universe. Go figure.

That alone makes you special if you can handle it. Absolutely amazing is your uniqueness. And everyone who influenced you were totally unique. You are the most unique of all the unique. Even horrible, tragic people are unique.

Your birth, your parents, your first kiss, your first child, your

You can be honest with yourself.

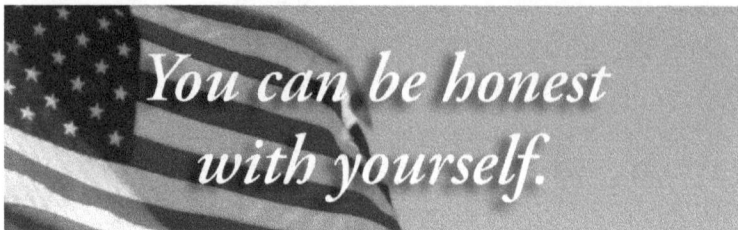

friends, your bosses, your doctors, and even your morticians are unique.

The challenge is to make your story unique in a good way. It is our choice to make decisions that will help someone or that will not help them. Unique choices that will affect unique people in unique ways. Choose to smile, to say "Thank You For Asking", choose to say "How may I help you?", choose to say "God Bless You", choose to be a good person.

Choosing to say "I'll have another drink" is not choosing.

It is losing.

It is time to prioritize our choosing.

Make sure the bad choices don't make the cut.

You see, your story is your glory.

Every Child

Every child is left behind when we don't teach them values.

Children are veins of gold in our future.

Rush the process and the mine crumbles.

How do you get 14kt gold to the jeweler and polished?

And then to the Fifth Avenue window for all to see its beauty?

It must be treated with care and respect to get defined as refined.

But our kids are being left in the mines. Families are burdened by disruption and schools with political correctness. What is best for the child is decided by committee, not parent… Not the teacher.

Teachers are remembered by kids for having been kind, nice, and caring… not for how well they followed the rules. Teachers are remembered for teaching what is good. But good is becoming a bad word as it might infer a value judgement. Now value judgement is what you wash the hog with.

Parents have to defer to the union. Teachers have to defer to the union. But the union now is really not a uniter. Sad semantics. But true.

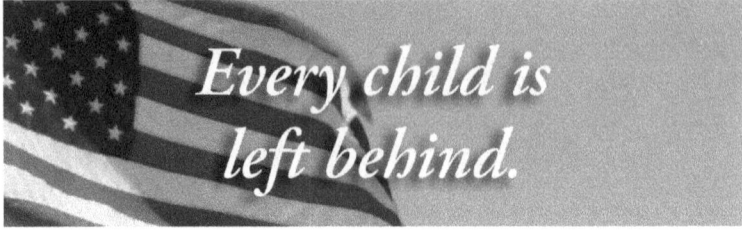

*Every child is
left behind.*

Putting aside unions what is the state of the union?

Is it on a values precipice?

Can anyone agree on what is good and what is bad, much less what is evil?

Are we dithering our future away?

Every child is watching.

Every child wants to be a setting for diamonds on a unique gold ring.

And not one in a pawn shop.

Your Six

Your six is what is directly behind you.

What you can't see.

Your vulnerable spot.

Your six means 180 degrees behind you.

Gotta check it out. Constantly.

Your back. Somebody has to protect your six, your back. Be it a wife or friend we always have to be on the lookout for one another. You go out on patrol and you need someone on your six.

Kids need someone looking out for them. You can't protect their six if you aren't there. Hello?

It is arrogant stupidity to not have someone watching your back. Things are said behind your back. Politics is a game of what goes on behind your back. We don't like people talking behind our back. That infers we should also not talk behind someone else's back.

"I never saw it coming." If you can say that, then you had no idea how much you were being talked about behind your back. That is

"I never saw it coming".

why we like people who are honest and up front. That is what we should be to be liked by others.

A wife is your best radar because they are so great at knowing everything anyone says about anybody. Take care of her and your six will be protected. LOL.

What do you think we have intelligence agencies for? To watch our country's back. This is serious back stuff. Real serious. Let them be. Abuse will always surface and punishment will be assigned. But don't tie the hands of our "backers"…

I can't imagine what it would be like being a black person who always is looking over his shoulder. Protection? Who to trust?

Families need their backs protected.

Nobody should be pushed from behind.

Hands

Palms up and you can read your future.

Clenched and you can break a nose.

Thumbs up is approval.

The index can point the way.

Middle finger…?

Hands can say a lot.

And, of course there is sign language.

Hand signals are critical in combat.

So hands really come in handy.

There is the fist bump. There is the shake. But most important is the clasp with fingers intertwined.

Looking eye to eye.

Black and white in a promise of peace.

Plastic

Plastic.

An industry that has penetrated every moment of our existence.

Just look at all the water bottles and plastic bags that are in landfills and oceans. From forks to flashlights to dashboards to vinyl siding.

You can never be more than 5 feet from plastic.

Plastic has altered the reach of man.

I bet plastic is now on the moon from the Apollo lunar landings.

We can't remain, but plastic can!

Plastic doesn't like fire but it is impervious to most other conditions.

Amazing stuff.

The one thing we have on it is that it is not alive. Except that it doesn't decay and lasts longer than we can. How long something lasts has become the new standard of mankind.

How long can Democracy last?

Plastic has altered the reach of man.

How long can poverty last?

How long can prejudice last?

How long will my eyesight last?

How long will I be able to help others?

Why do our dogs not last as long as us?

Especially when we need them……

Wait! We have an even newer use for plastic!! It might have been discovered in Beverly Hills. Hide the aging process. Enhance beauty. Nip, tuck, and chisel uniqueness away. And something more perfect emerges…. Except you can always tell….. It looks plastic.

Michael Jackson was even able to change color.

He didn't need to as his soul was so colorful. His beauty was his music, his color his pain. Why have we created notions that one has to look a certain way or be a certain color? Appearance being so important?

Why do I have to look the way I do? I am the ruler of my life and can do what I want. That right is protected in the Constitution. You can't regulate vanity. Ha!

The only thing which regulates vanity is poverty…

We change the faces of businesses. We market image. We will do anything to appear more likeable… from corporation to hot dog stand. Brilliant signs proclaiming excellence.

The front has become the back.

Who we really want to be is just our self.

This surgery can only be done inside.

Inside the heart where humility lies.

Where our original beauty can be shown with a smile and an outreached hand.

Now that is what I want to look like.

Get the Tan

I don't know for sure when it all started.

But sometime as a kid I met this Navy UDT guy and he had this tan.

He also had this neck chain with something on it.

I heard they had some joint in St. Thomas called the Silver Bullet... where frogs and stewardesses congregated and did the meringue ..... Tans were mandatory.

What is it about a tan? Girls sure look great in them.

Then there are the cruise ships of today. How do you walk the deck without tripping over a lounge chair? Why do hotels ruin the natural beauty with rows and rows of closely packed beach tanners? In Italy they have it down to a science. Good luck getting into the water.

I think the SEALs of today are so busy training and travelling that it is hard to find the few days to get The Tan. To them it is now a real luxury.

Who ever heard of a tan on a submarine? And the SEALs are the

Girls sure look great in them.

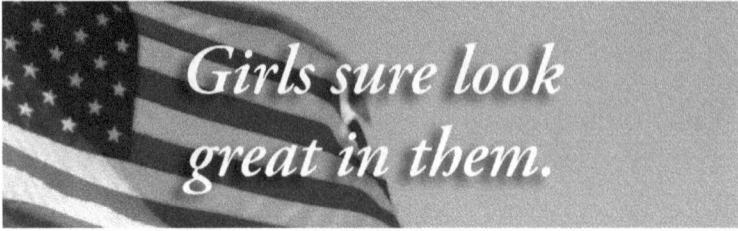

only ones to get topside ever so briefly before back in the water anyway....

A tan used to be a pseudo status symbol. Men who sailed and had yachts had them.

But.... you can't judge a man by the color of his skin.

Our greatest sin is judging others, looking for easy ways to form an intelligent appraisal from afar. Color is often the first filter. It is usually downhill from there.

How can you judge the substance of a man without knowing his heart?

Life can bring you humility and wisdom only if you discard ego and pride.

Only if you learn that helping others is the first act that defines one.

And helping not just your peers but anyone, even the dirty.

Yes, you can and should judge and attack evil.

But learning how to judge takes wisdom, commitment, and integrity.

You will make mistakes.

You will be chastised.

Too bad.

We have to learn the Way.

Wear Black

"Who died?"

You will get in big trouble if you don't wear black.

I gotta have a black tie and black suit and white shirt.

Should the tie be solid? … and the suit??

Maybe a pinstripe would be okay?

I bet there are some Hollywood type guys who will wear black shirts to be cool at someone else's death memorial.

Do my kids really have to wear black too? Is there a store that specializes in black, and when do they have sales??

Black is kinda scary. Who died anyway? Black makes it more scary. You know, cemetery scary. Glad they don't do these things at night.

Women really look absolutely fantastic in black. That's why I won't miss a funeral. Their hair looks great, their makeup looks great, their jewelry looks great, and their figure looks great. What's not to like? Plus they are usually in a sensitive, emotional zone and open for compliments and compassion. LOL.

"Who died?"

I like women in black. A black dress. Black stockings. Black heels. Black Chanel bag. Whatever.

Black also represents evil. Is there a tie-in here? Evil mocks and destroys the good of the world. White is good, black is bad. We all know this. White means pure.

Black the opposite. Black is associated with death.

Life must have some purpose, contrary to those who choose to elaborate otherwise. I just cannot give in to the idea that all is chance and we have no meaning after death. Who could look at the heavens and call it silly? Who could look at a child and call it evil? Every single person has been blessed with the gift of choice. Choose to believe and do anything you wish. There are always consequences. Now I choose to side with the good consequences. Now I choose to encourage the good, the unselfish, the humble, the white. "Now" was a long time coming, but it is here.

Test me. I dare you.

Darkness is created by man. The evil and injustice in this world is man's work. Man can undo bad, but there is a price. Today we would rather debate, posture, and assure rather than act. We have become afraid of evil. We are letting evil win. We are holding back and confusing the idealism of our youth. They want to serve good. We give them reasons and diversions not to. Social networking may be becoming their crutch and disabling philosophy.

Battles have to be fought.

We need soldiers not cellphones.

Hey, how did I get here??

"Who died?"

All I wanted to say was that women look fantastic in black.

Shimmering

Suppose a kid from your past told you that you made a big difference in their life?

That they found something to pursue that they could love because of you.

Would you not shimmer?

Don't we all want to shimmer?

To be modestly embarrassed by having done something good?

Is that not the reality show we want to watch? How about considering being a shimmer giver? That's what good teachers are supposed to do. I know one. He is black too. Color has nothing to do with shimmer.

Times Square has lights and signs that shimmer. That's fine for them. But we are talking about real shimmer.

That is an aura that surrounds someone who is known to be unselfish and caring. People whisper good things about them. The shimmerer never knows how far his shimmer reaches. Good travels fast in spite of bad getting all the media attention.

Don't we all want to shimmer?

Remember Peter Pan? Tinker Bell had a wand and a shimmer. She was always there to protect the Truth. The Truth could be that danger is near. In fact anything that is not Truth is danger.

We all are called to be guardians of the Truth. We are to call out lies and injustice. We are called to "wand" out every prejudice. Often it takes courage to stick your wand in someone else's face.

Are not men to protect family and Truth…..?

Isn't government meant to do the same?

Isn't bureaucracy supposed to insure this protection?

Don't tinker with my Liberty Bell.

Let the United States of America shimmer!

Evals

You go on a job interview and you get evaluated by some person who, for the moment, holds your life in their hands. Your grades so to speak.

Or it is review time and you are given your Evals… as we use to call them in the Navy.

It had to do with something like how hard you worked, but more often than not it was whether the person liked you.

As long as the system was fair it was ok. The threat of disapproval or economic punishment made one conscious of the requirements. There is some protection in systems of accountability.

In the old, old days it was just the mood of the owner of the business. He could be nice or rough and no one would know the difference. There was no media. No cell phones to text discrimination.

We have all been a slave to something. In its best form it is work that we love. We don't mind giving it all. Some people for money, some people for good.

But history had different cards to deal the blacks. Imported from Africa as a commodity to be sold into slavery to the highest bidder. Fear and servitude kept generations in pain and hunger. Labeled as a sub-class lower than a minority, their pride was chained to uncertainty. A prisoner to the white whim. Cheap labor took on a new meaning.

What a young child first experienced was a searing skepticism of honesty and fairness. Fear, when suppressed, will ultimately be passed on until the time when it can explode.

We are seeing in the 21st century that laws alone don't create order. Maybe we have to re-evaluate our approach? Or work harder at fairness. Protests are fine but helping your neighbor regardless of color is the real way to fight this war.

Guns will not be drawn by hands that have been held in honesty and compassion.

Every single one of us is needed to make the difference.

It won't happen otherwise.

I wonder what EVALS is spelled backward?

Lesson Plans

You have to plan what you teach…… kinda.

Maybe a plan shows intent just like a corporate mission statement, and you do this and that… as numbered events along the way.

But plans mean nothing if not used with creativity and spirit.

No one can ever predict all that can go wrong at the hands of Mr. Murphy. (Google Murphy's Law).

In every war there is a battle plan that becomes moot when the first shot is fired. Soldiers scramble for unplanned solutions. Lives are at stake. Triggers must be pulled. Plans be damned.

In every classroom the next hand raised can bring chaos and emotion. Students are kids… regardless of age… until they get out of school… (including you PHDs).

The period might be about Monet, Spanish, history…whatever… as long as values are not discussed??? Makes me think that a lesson plan is for the Principal to cover his fanny. I am ok with agreed upon guidelines, but the classroom is dynamic and shifts from moment to moment depending on how good the teacher is and how good the students are. Hire teachers with integrity and

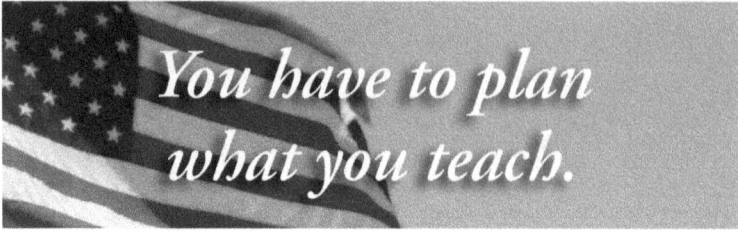

set them free. They are your men. You keep them from harm. They are more important than you.

Let the phantom complainers be treated with suspicion. Personal agendas have no plans. They should not be granted hidden official status.

You can't teach in a moral vacuum. It is the values and moralities that should be the understood framework for all teaching, be it art, history, politics, or science.

An incompetent teacher cannot teach values. Atheism must not be the god of academia. But it is. Because we are so lazy and so sensitivity-driven we have chosen to leave every child behind.

Lesson plans are fine if their objective is to create character in addition to knowledge. Character means integrity, humility, honesty, respect, and accountability.

So school boards… get off your dysfunctional dithering and face education head on.

Bring Love back to the classroom.

Love your teachers and let them love their students by giving everything they have in every moment.

Lesson Plans should allow the teacher to conduct a symphony that uplifts all.

Music teachers.

From single sheets of music, not bins of orchestrated reports.....

MIA

The POW/MIA flag has flown since the Vietnam War.

There is a lot of hidden politics regarding its history.

From America to China a lot of misinformation has stirred the emotion pot regarding those Missing In Action and Prisoners of War.

I think this flag has been flying for so long that it has enshrined a patriotic promise.

As a metaphor there is more here. We could ask .... Who is missing in action in our society? Or the world? Are we all prisoners? Of what war? The war of accountability?

This flag is only two colors. Black and White. Are we prisoners of black and white?

It is almost as if the tide has turned as the white is now dependent on the outcome of the black issue. Inverted prisoners of race.

What seems to be missing in action is Truth and Respect. They are being held in a faraway prison where compassion and values are being starved. Godless jailors keeping the lights off.

Are we prisoners of black and white?

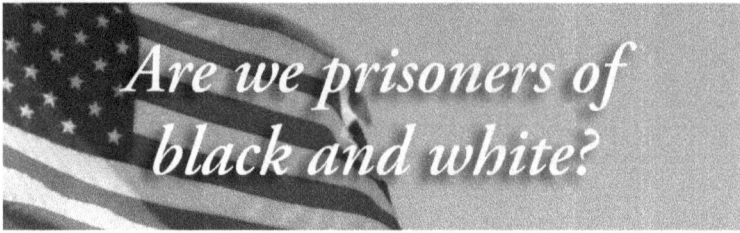

It will require special effort and Special Forces willing to risk their lives and face severe criticism.

The politics of political correctness has invaded all our schools and governments and stripped them of Faith in goodness and justice.

Christianity is mocked as an ideological joke by the left and others.

Laws have become so subservient to the sensitivities of political correctness that they confuse right and wrong, black and white.

Where are we going to find young people who are strong enough and morally fit enough to go behind these new enemy lines and risk their lives? Black and white side by side saying No to bias and dishonesty. Lives will be lost. Captives taken.

If we are not willing to risk as a nation then we will have given up on life, much less on our children and our families.

The young black man is missing in action.

He is a prisoner of the streets and disrespect.

We need him to be our future, not our past.

These are the front lines America....

Freedom is never free.

From sea to shining Thee.

Music

Ray Charles, Duke Ellington, Louis Armstrong, James Brown, Aretha Franklin, B.B. King, Whitney Houston, Michael Jackson, Ella Fitzgerald, Billie Holiday, Count Basie, Chuck Berry, Miles Davis, Little Richard, Chubby Checker, Kate Smith, Lionel Hampton, Harry Belafonte, and on and on.

You can't read this list and not have been touched.

Who taught them music?

I bet many were self-taught.

Why were we drawn to it when racism was so prevalent?

It was always the young who didn't like boundaries.

They just like what feels good, free, and honest.

We have a world that appears to be on the brink of self-destruction. Values are condemned. Women are abused. Children in slavery. Populations held in poverty. Education perverted. Governments bloated and dysfunctional.

Where does hope come from?? It still comes from music. Doesn't "Happy" just make you happy? In spite of everything? When

Ray Charles, Duke Ellington, Louis Armstrong…

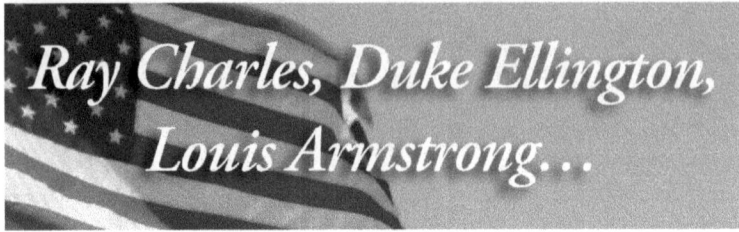

Whitney sang "I Will Always Love You" did your heart not stand still? Or when Aretha sings "Amazing Grace" is there not hope?

Today with Wi-Fi, Bluetooth, and cell phones, music goes everywhere. You can take a small Bluetooth speaker in your pocket into the heart of Iran and play the Star Spangled Banner… hope they let you take it to jail……

So when you look at how music has been shaped in the 20th century it was predominantly influenced by black musicians. Wow, that is a show stopper. How could white society not be in reverent gratitude? We have danced and moved to the beat of the black soul. Music integrated us before we even knew the word. It is such a shame that violence marred the journey.

Let's just say that the vestiges of racism are on the wane as the last flags are removed.

If we correct our past we can ennoble our future.

There are enormous challenges overseas that, if ignored, will bring a new blackness to all.

Unfettered atrocity must be addressed.

It is immoral to look away.

Play music in their cities and fields.

Plow music plow.

Save us again.

Soul Food

Way down south there was cooking that was rich and hearty made from almost everything nobody wanted.

Sharing was at the soul of soul food.

Tough times dictate sharing.

What feeds the soul, not the body, is the most important. Good in, good out. Think about it… Judging in, judging out. Gossip in, gossip out. Love in, love out. Truth in, truth out. Respect in, respect out.

What kind of food do you want your soul to have? Isn't it simple logic to want quality input into your soul, so it knows what the Truth is? To be able to see through half-truths and falsehood?

Somehow, because we can't see our souls…. Well, unless we look really honestly in the mirror… after the fogging clears…. LOL…. We dismiss soul as a part of our being and just let it be a description of a food and something in churches. We are paranoid about protecting our looks and our bodies. If they are good, we are good. Everyone will find us attractive…

Sharing was at the soul of soul food.

But you can't see trust or humility or real strength in a mirror. It can only be found in the eyes of others as they look at you. You can kinda sense what they may feel about you. And if you have been unselfish to them, it is easier to see. We exist if we have meaning to others. That meaning is all about your soul… your real heart… your real feelings and your real contribution. There is a lot to think about if you have any respect for yourself.

Maybe the hardest thing to cook is sole. It is a very light, white fish that is a delicacy if not over or under cooked. It can be so delicate that you almost don't notice it. Just like your soul.

Then there the soles on shoes.

Expensive shoes have expensive soles.

High heels put a lot of pressure on their soles.

Nike's have great comfortable soles.

More black people than any other race walk barefoot.

Open House

Sometimes the best way to sell a house is to make it available to anyone to see without a formal appointment.

Walk in and check it out without a pesky salesperson managing your thinking.

You can check out a lot of houses on a weekend that way and feel free.

Of course, if you are a seller you then cannot control who enters your front door.

Open house.

Kinda sounds right.

Open country. That is what we have been for a long time. Immigration was a controlled and fairly regulated process. Respect for our country, flag, and laws was the price of entry.

It worked for a while. Then we increased our demand for drugs and the borders became disrespected and porous. Like we brought it upon ourselves. Demand and crime go hand in hand. Shame on us.

So now our country is an open house.

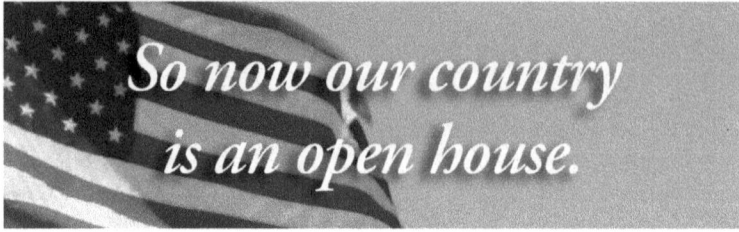

So now our country is an open house. You really don't need an appointment if you are willing to take the risk.

Hundreds of years ago slaves were brought across the borders illegally and we looked the other way. Injustice and economic imprisonment settled in.

Our culture had been enriched. We didn't know it. Today our culture's beauty is its diversity. We have come a long way. We have so many ancestors from European countries, African countries, and Asian countries and others. A porridge of embraced uniqueness.

No country has done better and done more for itself and the world. We have struggled with race and are still searching for an easy and legalistic solution. Amend this, amend that. Have the lawyers double check it. Add more pages to the explanation of how we should go forward.

But as you the reader really knows… deep down inside… the solution lies with each one of us acting as models of fairness and respect.

We must be examples of values held high.

Values that need not be written down.

Values that we embrace as who we are.

Come on, we all know the Truth.

Hate must abate.

Open House.

Fixer-Upper

Find the most rundown house in a better neighborhood and buy it for a song and fix it up.

Miracles can happen with a little imagination and effort.

Habitat For Humanity.

Habitat For Self.

The smiles of gratitude are the most rewarding of them all. Any time you help someone else. Anytime. Every time.

Every home can use a little fixer-upping. Paint a new color on one wall. Add a window to bring light in.

Every heart can use a little fixer-upping. Paint one wall white, then one wall black, then one wall grey, or yellow, or blue, or aqua, or ……. Or, change the color of the trim or windows. And afterwards clean it real good.

Clutter shows disrespect for self. Neatness and cleanliness shows respect for self and others, and that you may be somebody. Poverty does not mean not to have respect. Look at all who were given nothing in childhood, not even a parent. But with

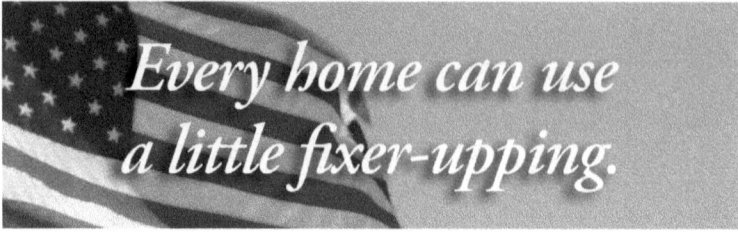

values and a positive step they climbed the ladder of self-worth. Regardless of color.

These fixed-up people are our silent leaders. We need them not to be silent but to share their story so we can be fixer-uppers.

After you fix up a house it is worth so much more than the effort and cost put into it. So we can be worth more.

So consider fixing up just one friend. Just one stranger. Just one African-American.

Hammer, saw, nails, wood, paint, and sweat feel good when doing good. Funny how the house and you get fixed up. Sweat equity in another human being.

Oh what the heck, do it for the worst house in the worst neighborhood.

It will plant a seed even if it burns.

Seeds grow and become fixer-uppers where they are planted.

We all notice when someone does something right.

Fix me up I want to fly.

Back of the Bus

What would it feel like to be told to go to the back of the bus?

Or to walk into places with signs saying "blacks only"?

Institutionalized unworthiness.

Looking down one's nose at someone.

It's called arrogance, ignorance, and cruelty.

That simple.

It has existed since the beginning of cultures. There were always the lower classes and slaves on every continent. Where the only light in these cultural dungeons was hope and faith.

But from there rose the greatest of men and women. Those who knew pain and injustice. Who could look one straight in the eye in Truth. Who in the world would choose to be a Mandela?

There is an invisible bus in every corporation and organization and town and city. It takes a heart with insight and compassion to see these busses. This is the terrain of the courageous. How about spiritual SEALs? You don't have to run and swim miles and miles. You don't have to have muscles. You can even be in a wheelchair

Looking down one's nose at someone.

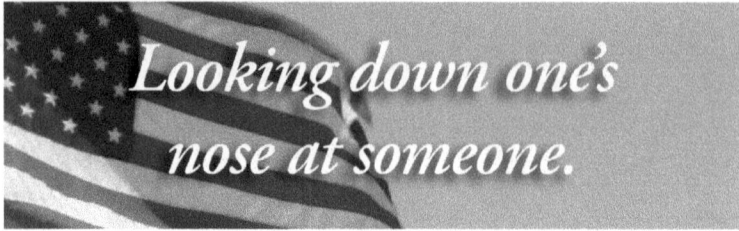

and show the path to the Truth. You can encourage and console. Sincerity and humility helps guide kids out of the back of the bus.

It's great to ride in the bus in New York City. No one is the same. All pay the same fare. All get off at different stops. There really is no back. Doors open at both ends.

There is a bus that leads somewhere.

That takes you to where you really want to go.

The fare is humility and respect for others.

The fare is one unselfish act before you get on and after you get off.

Then you can ride that bus every day and get to where you were meant to go.

You will be greeted by thousands when you finally get off.

They all will be smiling.

State Police

It is stated that we must have police to maintain law and order and fairness...

If intruders into our homes and into our businesses and into our lives can come and go at will... then there is no reason to live.

So we have laws and a structure to enforce those laws.

They hold for all... rich and poor.

The police did not create poverty, nor make the laws. The police do not create crime. People do. Police are told to be as fair as possible under the laws.

There are city police, state police, federal police, international police, and our military police. These men give up normal 9-5 lives and put themselves in harm's way to protect us.

The problem is us, not them.

We need to be retrained to be respectful and moral. Welfare has not made us better, it has enabled disrespect and laziness. In principal it is good, but not when administered by enormous bureaucracy. It has become a cultural cancer. The silliness of fake

The police did not create poverty.

job application routines to fulfill welfare requirements is absurd. There is no follow-up by these desk ridden fiefdoms. It is not possible. And they are overpaid.

You make much more on welfare than on entry level jobs….

State Police.

God bless them.

What is the state of police?

They have become the bad guys. Morality is no longer a politically correct notion. Values are no longer taught in schools. Sensitivities and feelings and opinions yelled are more potent. Media does not embrace good as much as it does bad. Protest is truth before it's protested by logic.

We do not have a Police State.

We, yes we, need reprimands and leadership more so than the police.

Martin Luther King made more impact than any other leader. How?

Are there not any new gifted leaders who can lead with values?

Disagreement does not have to be disrespect.

Manners are required of us and Congress.

What is the state of leadership?

Don't ask too much of the State police.

Adam Bomb

How do we know what color Adam was?

Well, it really doesn't matter.

What did matter is that he bit the nuclear apple and we are left with the fallout.

I won't blame woman.

"The devil made me do it" defense works for me.

Adam made a choice. Every one of us makes a choice. To do good or to disrespect it. Good intentions don't count.

The fallout of everything we do can strengthen or weaken someone, including one's self. A lie can be a bomb to the deceived. Selfishness distances one from the trust of others.

We strive for accomplishments so we can be known for something. You can run a marathon. You can fool a policeman. You can get on welfare. You can be a nurse or doctor. You can swim a mile. You can go to church.

Everyone describes another person by their accomplishments be they good or bad. We all want to be respected. But respect only

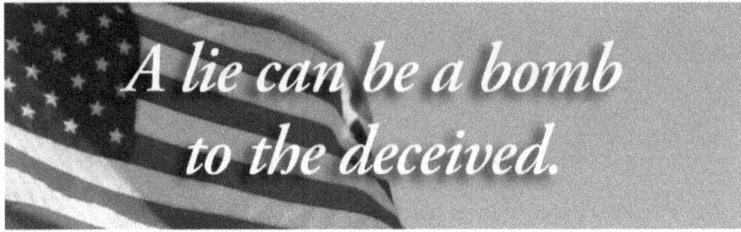

comes from honesty, compassion, integrity, humility, and trust. Do these qualities describe you?

We, like Adam, have big choices to make even though they appear to be no bigger than an apple. We choose to dismiss consequences as being minimal.

The child hears or sees it. A message has been sent. He is in your class for that moment and you have taught the lesson. Except your lesson plan has no value if it is not about values.

We think we are not that important. But the Truth is that we are. Affect one other person's life in a positive way and that medal sits on your chest for life and thereafter. I don't know how some good people walk upright with the weight of all the medals they have earned. Hunching with pride is more beautiful than standing straight with vanity. The mirror may see muscle, but the heart only sees good.

So we make a choice every hour of every day.

Helping one person insures there is no radiation.

If we are selfish the hospitals will overflow.

Truth Lies

How do we ever know the Truth?

So many lies are told and they aren't true.

Half-truths are lies.

The whole truth and nothing but the truth so help you God.

Chiseled into Federal buildings is the word Truth.

Except that we no longer want the Truth. We are more drawn to statistics and polls. Data and feelings.

Statistics lie. They strip the qualitative from the discussion. They strip our qualities from us. I am not a number.

Someone sent me an e-mail about the number of unarmed civilians killed versus police killed. This was to be about race. Well, duuhh, the police are armed and not apt to be killed, and the circumstances of the unarmed are not figured in... were they on drugs, or violent..??

We are bombarded with statistical analysis by geniuses pounding keyboards. Detached??

Half-truths are lies.

And, the opinion polls. Who and how asks what questions at what time of what demographic? Are we being led by idiocy?

We the people can read between the lines and are getting even better at it. It is a sad time when what we are being told is the truth is a lie.

Our nation was founded on certain Truths. We have fought wars over them and now have a new war to bring Truth back into our lives, nation, and family.

The Truth lies in a politically and statistically incorrect notion of what is moral.

The answer lies in doing good. Help someone. Promote and stand up for values. So the child can learn by watching us…. Not from a video game.

A war has to be agreed upon. Lies must be exposed and ridiculed.

Social networks are the new bloodless army. A billion young adults saying "no more lies" about the truth. Viral exposures of falsehood have the power to bring governments and injustice to their knees. Even bureaucracies which hide behind the lies buried in their reports. Cannot the truth of women's rights be brought to the fore? Cannot child abuse be called for what it is? Cannot every nuance of racism be identified?

We have to begin to trust the Truth again.

How do you recognize it among all the lies?

Wherein does It lie?

The Book is black.

All Black

Suppose we all were black.

No white. No color. Just black.

No more racism.

French blacks, Italian blacks, Russian blacks, Iranian blacks, Chinese blacks, etc.

A world where color is no longer an issue.

What then would we find to divide us?

All police are black. All politicians are black.

All births are black. All deaths are black.

All prayers are black.

There is a New Zealand Rugby team called the All Blacks. They win and win. They win because they hold integrity, commitment, and practice to the highest of standards. No politics. Just truth. Each player is held to account. Misbehavior and misplaced ethics means you cannot belong to the team. The notion of team becomes paramount. You take care of one another. You get so

close that you can anticipate the other. Spontaneous decisions in the moment determine the win. Leadership and learning are taught to all.

As you look into this example of success you see that high standards must be met to excel. Most don't want to pay this price for excellence. Excellence is earned by repetition and pain. Self-pushed into world of no self. Serving the team and your fellow player pushes success.

So as a nation of all blacks we have to demand high standards of ourselves. Teach and preach them from birth to grave. Values that are good and right. Values we know are there and one's we so often ignore in the moment.

When all us blacks are good and unselfish, peace will be within reach.

Governments and bureaucracies and regulations can function with strict values. Sadly, they inefficiently pander to political correctness and insecurities…. And waste lives. But man has a funny way to deny himself what he needs. We create prejudices just to feel important…. Or something??

Just an exercise in color.

It's science fiction…

And a film that will never be made.

Unless it is in black and white?

Care Package

I don't care.

Leave me alone.

I have enough problems.

Go away.

Enough problems is the "me". The "I's" have it....

Until one learns that you have no problems when you are helping others. Duuuhhh? Why don't we get it??

Care packages show someone, be it family or stranger in some foreign country, or a person in the military that you care... Care packages can be food, toys, books, batteries, toothpaste, or any kind of gift. So there can be 1,000's of types of care packages.

For the most part we send care to people we don't know. If we could put a face of a specific individual on it we would send even more. We really want to help a real person. It's just not set up that way. It's impersonal.

There are care packages you can send that are not material. Let's label them private/heartfelt communications. PHC's.

We don't care how you package it.

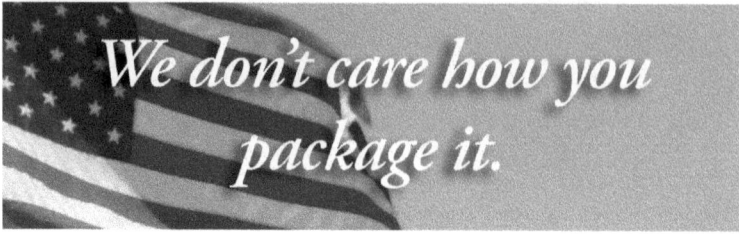

When someone knows you care about them…both of you feel good. Simple. Powerful. We don't get it.

Helping someone is a kind of care package. And so fun to send. And cheap. No postage or shipping charges. Some people you send lots of PHC's to. Others, one, once in a while. But every time you conceive one you get excited by the anticipation of giving it! It's true!

Love is a care package when it is humble and genuine.

I think our governments need to send us care packages of reduced spending, reduced administrative confusion, reduced political correctness, reduced inefficiency, reduced fine print, and on and on.

But nobody trusts anybody.

So maybe there could be a trust care package?

We don't care how you package it. Just get it delivered in half the time for starters. How about a politician's care package? Get the same health care and benefits as a normal citizen and put every contribution on every cell phone so we all can see it all the time.

I'd love a care package that protected small business and churches.

I'd like a package where minorities don't rule.

I'd like a package where feelings don't trump logic.

If we care about our country and our world let's start to care more.

Oneness

What does it feel like to be one?

The only one.

Or just one, not two?

One reporting to no one.

If... you are the only one.

It is just a number unless it is you.

For one means nothing unless there are two.

Why is it that we always pursue two?

We need another to make us whole. Man and woman. To make more.

In two can there be unity? That is what love tries to do. To make us one.

One world? One nation?? One family?

The world is horrifically divided. Yet from orbit it is one beautiful blue and white sphere... A visual paradise. Floating in an infinite blackness.

What does it feel like to be one?

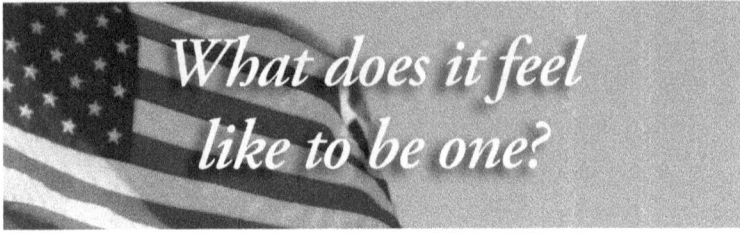

Our nation is divided. The United States of America. The pinnacle of man's achievement and potential to date. The USA had made freedom her song. She is paying a painful price trying to manage it all. Oneness has become elusive. We even have two parties doing a great job of preventing unity.

We are addicted to the feeling of love. We want it. The delusion is the need for drugs to create the euphoric feeling of false love's presence. We love this, we love that. We love Love. But only in unity is love found. We don't get it.

Doing something unselfish for another is Love. It feels so good. Gratitude is erotic.

We should be grateful for our nation. For being blessed to live here. It is the blessing to count.

Yet…. we wallow in disunity and criticism. Our choice. But if every one person reached their hand out….???

Two's would be joined.

Unities would spread.

Slums would disappear.

Oneness would be two smiles.

God Bless America.

We need it.

How about a one star flag?

Why Bother

I don't care.

Leave me alone.

I have enough problems.

Go away.

Same old. Same old. Don't bother me. I am busy and I have my job and family to provide for. Enough is enough with all these issues. Racism? That's their problem. I didn't have anything to do with it.

The police on the streets only come out when there is danger to property and people. Let them do their job and I can watch it on the evening news. I'd rather watch the commercials than another tragic ending.

Why bother?

The world sees our racial strife and notes that this purportedly great democracy cannot solve it. So our influence in the world is diminished by our own hypocrisy.

What is the cause of racism? Prejudice. Exactly what our

I have enough problems.

Constitution was written to solve. It is our execution that disassembles it.

Are we the largest user of drugs?? Why?? This great nation? Media and film that panders to the outrageous?

Why bother? Well, if we don't, the seeds of our demise will sprout even more and the evil abroad will have a field day.

We have to bother.

We have to bother those who do wrong and who talk wrong. They can bother us… why can't we bother them??? If they are immoral why can't we be moral??? Bother me and I have a right to bother you.

Bureaucracy and voice prompts bother me. They are making it harder and harder to bother back.

So vote for new leaders who can't be bothered by bother.

We all should refuse to sign documents that are more than 200 words.

Heck, The Ten Commandments are less than 100.

Why bother reading them?

Helps Outreach

There are some people out there who don't like to be bothered by poverty or misfortune.

They see faces of all colors, including black and white.

It is a colorless business as you don't have the time to think about such nonsense anyway.

This couple got this stupid notion that helping others gave more meaning to their lives than helping selves. And that helping others provides the biggest reward and smile you can get.

You and I know it is a bother to be bothered by other people's circumstances. Let the government handle it with their costly inefficiencies. Report after report enlightens the unenlightened.... After breaks.... LOL

Let's take our nation into our own hands. One individual at a time.

Youth love to help others if we show them how and provide the means. Why? Because they feel it is right. Go figure?

Reaching out is the only way to eliminate our image as hypocritical. We hide behind our social worlds and make our donations to manage bother.

Anyone can come in the front door.

Helps Outreach is actually the name of a non-profit that started from zero in a humble space and began getting food and furniture and clothing donated and organized.

Anyone can come in the front door. Anyone.

But you have to take off your sunglasses and look them straight in the eye. A prayer is offered. Mind boggling in simplicity and power.

They have one truck now… painted with the Helps Outreach logo and phone number. I call it the "Bother" truck because it bothers your conscience. It's not about fancy dinners at the Ritz…. No time for that. Too many people need us to bother them.

Outreach means reaching out… and going to the front lines.

This is hypocrisy combat.

Under the radar and kinda covert.

I like that.

No racism here.

No time for it.

Hand Out

A hand out is not a handout.

This is where we got lost along the way.

We depersonalized that which was meant to be personal.

We gave everything to government.

Off our backs onto its.

Government, by the way, is an "it". We aren't.

Handout is a word associated with the need of another.

A hand out is a reaching to put a face on help.

Fingers intertwined, not of the same color is needed.

Every black person should find a white hand to grasp.

Every white person should find a black hand to grasp.

Problem solved.

Think about it.

EPILOGUE

I have been blessed with a journey that has not seen the real poverty or felt the real pain of the majority. Please don't judge me by the immaterial, much less the material. I was born in Bronxville, NY in 1940. Grew up in Louisville and St Louis. Graduated from Yale and went into the Navy. I had the great honor of fulfilling my dream to become a Frogman. I graduated from BUDS Class 31E, Basic Underwater Demolition/Seal Training. I was an officer in Underwater Demolition Team 21 which became Seal Team 4 in 1984. I had the honor of recovering several spacecraft, including Gemini 6/7 & AS-201, the very first Apollo Spacecraft to go into space. Wow, did I luck out. Then I spent 40 years in women's retail, in various department stores. Even a year at the World Wrestling Federation... go figure?

I have two great daughters and two grandchildren who have just discovered the water and facemasks. My wife has created probably the #1 women's accessory store in the country as evidenced by how much she is copied. Therein I work and report to her... No comment. LOL.

As you can tell by reading between the lines there is a spiritual side to my journey. Kind of covert as I just want to make a difference unseen.

God Bless You All... Happy Trails.

ACKNOWLEDGEMENTS

I wrote this book a good while ago…. Not knowing when to release it. The events of this year have me saying it is time. This is a caring attack on racism and an attempt to recognize the dignity and potential of black America.

The politics of generations have not brought us to the place we had hoped for. I am just one white man who is honored to have some long-term black friendships. I draw on this and all of our discussions over the years and am trying to look at our challenges through a respectful lens.

This is about the sensitivities needed to discern the solution to the challenges of diversity. All diversities.

The chapters average only 300 words. There is no planned order. You can open the book anywhere and read a 2 page chapter and get a smile and a frown… hopefully they will also cause you to think.

Maybe these books will be found some day and will help future generations make fewer mistakes. Isn't 1-800 where you go for help…that is free??

I have to always acknowledge those who make a difference to me. This is the short list.

There are my daughters, Candice and Courtney, who thought

they knew their dad, but really didn't. There is my brilliant wife Christina, who thought she knew her husband..... And then there are my friends from the past whose life journeys I do not fully know, and who do not know me now. For in life it is who we become, not who we were.

Then there are the men of my "No Walls" Bible Studies and Max Lucado who freed us to think with assurance and humility, leading me to new friendships of the highest quality.

There are the veterans I served with and those I didn't. Ames, Riojas, Stevens, Cleary, Fry, Ross, Hawes, Hawkins, Bisset, Hernandez, Bruton, Olson, Vecchione, Phillips, Waddell and my brothers in BUD/S 31E, and countless others … where bonding and trust was defined.

Lastly, there are Sandra Simmons-Dawson and Brian Dawson who helped edit and format the books, website, and marketing. Their firm, Money Management Solutions, Inc. dba Customer Finder Marketing http://customerfindermarketing.com/ is a gem.

IN THE WORDS OF OTHERS

Reviews for 1-800-Only-For-Love

"I started reading 1-800-Only-For-Love. I have put it down only to let you know how powerful I think it is. Just half way through it and it brings tears to my eyes, chapter after chapter. I cannot tell you how much it mirrors my life.

We have often spoken about personal feelings and events in our lives and how similar they are. This book tells it all. What we have given up over the years in order to advance ourselves. Turning our backs on Love when really it has been what we lost, what we needed, and what we were searching for, even today.

I want to give my daughters, daughters-in-law, Ex-wife, and current roommate/girlfriend a copy to read. It says a lot that I cannot express for myself. Thanks and God Bless.

Lee Lyons – Naples, FL

Reviews for 1-800-For-Veterans-Only

"I will always have a special place in my heart for our veterans. Growing up in a military family, I spent my childhood years living on various Air Force bases, learning the lingo, and exploring the far corners of the world while my father flew various missions in both peacetime and conflict. This upbringing has given me a love and appreciation of anything written about the military, whether it be a Tom Clancy thriller or a World War II biography. Author Chris Bent has written some wonderful books in the past few years and I simply love his latest, "1-800-For-Veterans-Only".

Bent definitely has a way with words and his short essays on a variety of topics are conversational, often very witty, and sometimes quite touching. There are so many things that are touched on in this read that it would be impossible not to strike a chord with someone who has had any connection to the military over their lifetime, myself included. From thoughts on enlisting, experiences at boot camp, early days in the service and the uncertainties faced, to the battleground itself. Bent discusses not only what it's like to come home after a deployment, but the experiences of being a veteran and some of the darker aspects of this that we see in our country today.

One of the things that I found most inspiring about Bent's latest was his ability to speak directly to those veterans who may be out there and possibly struggling. There is some very sage wisdom in this one and it certainly has the potential to turn some lives around. Very well done."

TFL READER – Amazon Book Reviewer

A Veteran's Comment on the Chapter "The Hand"

"I agree because when this USMC veteran returned home there were no handshakes or high fives but plenty of shaken fists.

I'm reminded of a verse from "Where No One Stands Alone"

"Hold my hand all the way every hour every day

From here to the great unknown

Take my hand let me stand

Where no one stands alone."

There are two photos of hands representing two distinct eras:

The first is a stained glass window in a Chapel at Paris Island. S.C., with The Hand of God holding 12 Marines from my unit who were killed on Jan. 20, 1968 in Quang Tri Province, Vietnam.

The second is a marble work entitled "Hand in Hand" that stands at the entrance of a children's rehabilitation clinic in Dong Ha, Vietnam, just a few miles from the site where the above Marines were killed."

Floyd Killough, USMC (Ret.)

Reviews For 1-800-Oh-My-Donald

No matter what your politics are...

I love an interesting read that stretches my beliefs and makes me think. I have found that author Chris Bent has the ability to do just that and to entertain at the same time as I have read several of his books in the past year. His latest, "1-800-Oh-My-Donald" is a great play on Trump's run for the brass ring, but it is also much more than that. In his series of short chapters and essays, Bent gives his thoughts on The Donald but also on the state of the world, racism, evil, feminism, happiness, and even Hillary. Another well-written and most interesting read from Bent. Definitely recommend.

TLF Reader – an Amazon Top 500 Reviewer
Another blast of wit and humor

Having read almost any other book by Chris Bent ('1-800-I-AM-Unhappy' popped my cherry to the unique wit and humor Bent has been known for), I knew that at the get-go, '1-800-Oh-My-Donald' is going to be like a missile that hits you in the heart. What I love about Bent's writing is the sheer absence of pretention—Bent doesn't have any affectation, no high-brow attempts at appearing like some expert. Bent is just being himself, and he draws upon the deep well of personal experiences to write these what you may call "flash essays."

This book revolves around Donald Trump and the upcoming elections. But it would be a mistake to simply think that this book is an endorsement of Donald Trump nor is it exclusively about Trump—in fact, this book is an invitation to wonder and think about the many unspoken ponderables that strike us whenever election season comes— what is it are we really looking for, and is any of our ideas realistic or grounded in reality? What makes certain candidates tick? Why do we believe in promises? And what do we really want?

Bent's wry sense of humor and dead-pan observations pours down on you like a bucket of warm water—it is an entertaining read, like listening to the older guy hanging around at the train station. Or a kindly uncle who has been around the world and back and has a ton of things to tell you. These are pieces here that brought a tear to my eye, such as the one titled "She Works Hard." In any case, I love this book for its timeliness and for Bent's effort in collecting some of the most important morsels of wisdom from his past books. If you read the first 10 pages and you liked it, then you must realize this is also a great gift to loved ones. Highly recommended to readers of all ages!

Meghan – Amazon Reviewer
Very entertaining

I also personally find it refreshing to find an author that isn't afraid to add some humor to the current political times and situation and lighten up the mood a little bit. It seems that most people these days tend to take everything far too seriously, even much more so that the current political climate warrants. On that note, I also must say that author Chris Bent has a genuinely unique and entertaining sense of humor – it's not often that I find myself laughing out loud while reading a book, so I was quite surprised to find myself doing so several times throughout the read.

As well as this, all humor aside, the author still manages to raise some important points for discussion and debate, and he has definitely left me not only entertained, but also with a few things to ponder upon and think about more in the future. Overall, I enjoyed the read and it has given me a great first impression of the author. I highly recommend 1-800-Oh-My-Donald for any readers looking for an original and unique political commentary that I personally consider to be a more than worthwhile read.

Lucidity – Amazon Reviewer

Reviews for 1-800-For-SEALS-Only

"Pungent, cogent, wistful, idealistic, naive, wise, — all in no particular sequence, reflecting a view of life that it is all unpredictable, and it is mental, physical & moral preparation that will sustain us... there are life lessons and observations here for anyone and everyone...."

Lt (jg) James Hawes, BUDS 29E, SEAL, CIA,
(He was the First SEAL In Africa)...(sadly was my UDTR Instructor too)

"Who knew SEALs could write? (LOL) But what Chris does with his gift is really less "writing" than it is expressing the "unwritten." We all have our thoughts; and Frogmen have certain very special and unique shared experiences. Chris puts the pen to the task of relating what we (the Frogs) have experienced and what we (all of his readers) now observe in sharing the experience of the world around us. It's challenging and funny (if you've been through a "real Hell Week"), and sometimes sad. But hey, isn't life? Hooyah!"

Timothy Phillips, SEAL, BUDS 166, ST-8, ST-4

"Chris - great stuff...as always. "Hooyah Mike"..."Every sin is a grenade"..."My wife is my swim buddy"...great thoughts as only a SEAL can put into words. I love it and will BUY a few copies for my Assistant Sergeant at Arms to read to guide their young lives... Hooyah Chris and see you soon!"

Phil King, Sergeant at Arms, NC Senate, BUDS 32

"Mr. Bent's words of wisdom on some of the evolutions of U. S. Navy SEAL training are demonstrated to apply to everyday life with such simplicity. God, Family, Country, is the essence of being an honorable and patriotic American. It is the ethos of the Navy SEAL credo. The band of brothers whose lives are bonded as one in being; all for one and one for all! Nothing in this world feels better to receive in life as the emblem, the SEAL Trident, of a true warrior and to receive into one's heart the holy trinity! Hooyah! The only easy day was yesterday!"

Erasmo Elijah Riojas (Doc Rio) HMC (SEAL) Ret.

"I am a SEAL Teammate of LT. Chris Bent. During our years of serving our country as Naval Special Warfare Operatives, Chris always manifested that "Can Do" attitude so necessary for success in what many would consider: "A tough way to make a living!"

Among other sub-specialties, Chris and I had the honor of being the Platoon Commanders who would "Recover Astronauts!" Within the pages of "1-800-FOR-SEALS-ONLY", you will get to see the mind-set of students going through BUDS Training (still the toughest Military Training in the World) with most Classes experiencing an over 80% Drop Out Rate! Chris masterfully combines our training to current issues existing today. A Giant HOOYAH for a must read publication! 1-800-FOR-SEALS-ONLY is awarded a big BRAVO ZULU from your old Teammates!"

Dr. Frank Cleary, OIC, Seventh Platoon, ST-2 (Ret.)

"Five Stars for the FROGFATHER! This is a great book, and should be required reading...."

Commander (SEAL) Tom Hawkins, USN, Ret., author, NSW Historian

"Chris Bent has again taken his many and varied life experiences and applied them to life in general and "how to do it right". This book is clearly for everyone, not just SEAL's. Life was never meant to be easy and all of us can take away something from this book and the Frogman saying "The only easy day was yesterday". Even if it is the hard way....do the right thing.

From one Frogman to another I say to Chris, your eulogy (chapter 75) should be read when the time comes: Teammate, seen or unseen, you truly have made a difference!

Hooyah 1-800-For-SEALS-Only!"

Mike Macready, SEAL Team One, BUD/S 49 West Coast

"Chris Bent's latest 1-800 offering certainly gets my SEAL of approval...
Using his own unique blend of insight, intellect and inspiration, Chris
lifts parallels from the rich history and tradition behind the US Navy
SEALs to provide challenging questions and equally thought provoking
answers to this experience that we call life. In this social-networking,
politically-corrected day and age where common sense, discipline and
values seem to have fallen by the wayside, Chris Bent cuts through like
a K-Bar to remind us all exactly what is of the utmost importance."

Darren A. Greenwell - NSW Historian, Researcher, Collector

Reviews for 1-800-Oh-My-Goodness

"With 1-800-Oh-My-Goodness, Chris Bent offers his thoughts on a
variety of topics, in order to amuse, inspire, and challenge any reader.
With his witty insight, and perspective forged from life experience,
Chris seeks to help us all become better individuals."

Michael Hopkins, Attorney, Naples, FL

"In this book Chis is honest and open with the reader. He definitely
gives you a lot to ponder. You can't wait to see what he is going to share
next."

Dorothy K. Ederer O.P., Director of Campus Ministry, St. John Student Center

"Oh my goodness", Chris has again presented a faith filled and thought
provoking book. His stream of thought, that often reads more like
poetry than prose, will cause you to rethink moments of life in a context
of love and promise."

Rev Jean Moorman Brindel, CFRE, AFP, Associate Director of
Development, Emeritus United Theological Seminary, Dayton Ohio

"Honest, incisive, poetic and profound: the writings of Chris Bent.
Passion for people, the nation and the world spring from his pages;
provocative questions leap from the shortest chapters ever. Silent voices
speak in these pages and nothing is to be taken for granted, for life and
love run deep between the lines of 1-800-Oh-My-Goodness."

Wendy J. Deichmann, PhD, President, United Theological Seminary

Reviews for 1-800-Laughing-Out-Loud

"Chis is a stew: meat, potatoes, veggies, gravy, biscuits and mustard. A warm, tender mix of good taste, generous servings, and something for all appetites! Chris mixes a Hunter S. Thompson "Gonzo Journalism" writing style with a Soupy Sales "Pie in the Face" sense of humor. Chris writes about: Life Values, Family, Self, Respect, Good & Evil. His perspective of life's Value Proposition engages our brain to think about ourselves and others. Chris' previous books are from the Heart and Soul. Take his counsel of his life's experience. There is good advice in each chapter! You will enjoy each word like every bite of a good stew."

Gerry Ross, Executive, Pratt & Whitney (Retired)

"Chris Bent is the type of guy you want to share a cold beer with at the end of a lousy day and have him philosophize on the real meaning of life. Since you might not have that opportunity anytime soon let me suggest you read 1-800-LAUGHING-OUT-LOUD. Perfect title for the book, because when reading it you will."

Nancy Lascheid, RN, BSN, Co-Founder, Neighborhood Health Clinic, Naples, Florida

Reviews for 1-800-For-Women-Only

"It is amazing that a man would want to write about women. That is a change, but Chris has a sense of humor that can make you laugh. Women will enjoy this book and men may gain new insight."

Dorothy K. Ederer, O.P., Director of Campus Ministry,
St. John Student Center, East Lansing, Michigan

"Light, refreshing take on some not so light topics. Wrapped in silliness and wit are serious, social and moral truths that challenge us to be more than ordinary."

Peggy Ryba, Membership Director, North Naples Church, Naples, Florida

"Chris is like a modern day prophet, throwing modern day concepts and concerns out there for us to contemplate. The seeds he tosses can land on sand or soil depending on the reader. I suggest you pull up a nice spot in your garden and sit down and read…then allow some of his thoughts to germinate in your life! "

Mia Guinan, Owner, Gourmet Gang, Camp Trident, Virginia Beach VA

"1-800-For-Women-Only or the "Mystery of Women" is interesting because it is brutally accurate. In fact, it is frightening to read the explanations of characteristics of women. Many of these things I had not even been aware of, but they are "right on target". The book is written with great sensitivity and insight. I never got the feeling that women were criticized, but accepted as observed. It is an easy fun read and a great gift to give to a friend or even a son who is even thinking of getting married. As the mother of three sons, I know it is true; "Heartfelt is at the core of being. Being somebody."

Sue Lester, Volunteer, Children's Coalition of Collier County,
Pilot Club, Naples, Florida

"Chris Bent's extraordinary life has given him a perspective that so very few have. His insight comes not only from his incredible experiences but from his deeply rooted sense of responsibility, caring, and love for others. His thoughtful mind is not on idle, but instead always on overdrive, crystallizing in well thought out words those concepts that would have many times escaped us, were it not for the efforts of this author to engage, care deeply, and then, as Chris has done so remarkably here, write."

Jennifer L. Whitelaw, Attorney, Whitelaw Legal Group, Naples, FL

Reviews for 1-800-I-Am-Unhappy (Volumes 1 and 2)

"This is a book by a man of many directions and passions. Straightforward yet thought provoking. Loyal to his convictions and country. And brave. Sharing. Warrior. Humanitarian."

Jeff Lytle, Editorial Page Editor, Naples Daily News

"As a friend, Chris has helped me understand the inherent conflicts embedded in the language of 'political correctness' and how it attempts, and frequently succeeds, in disguising and defeating the 'truth.' Chris is engaged in a rhetori- cal battle — we need his insight."

William Lord, a 32-year-veteran Executive Producer and Vice-President of
ABC News, and Professor of Journalism at Boston University

"Chris writes like he lives. As a man of distinction, he is a voice for the poor, a champion of the truth and a friend of strong character and conviction. His word and his service are a blessing to all who encounter him."

Vann R. Ellison, President/CEO, St. Matthew's House, Inc.

"My nickname for Chris is "Dream-Catcher"- because that's who he is to me. He is my mentor in how to give on His behalf. Freely and generously, Chris offers both words, "God bless you!", and gifts. And all the while he is making a compelling and powerful statement. Chris Bent has discovered a beautiful way to live!"

Rev. Dr. Ruth Merriam, The Church on the Cape (U.M.C.), Cape Porpoise, Maine

"Chris Bent is a very unusual person – Navy SEAL, Yale graduate, successful business owner, and radical Christian who is comfortable talking with anyone at any level in society. He doesn't just talk about faith or caring about the poor, Chris actually lives his faith and he works with the poor. His smile is genuine and reflects his deep joy in life, America, hard work, people and (most definitely) God. I have enjoyed reading his writings; they are different, often hard hitting and sometimes maybe even a little wild. Each one gives a fresh perspective on contemporary lives, reflecting Chris' intel- ligence and faith. Chris enjoys moving mountains."

Rev. Dr. Ted Sauter, Senior Pastor, North Naples United Methodist Church